Heart Work

How to live, love, and lead
from the inside out

Heart Work Leadership Group

"Heart Work positions those of us who have the agency to design a safe environment where teams can be introspective, vulnerable, and open about matters of life, love, and leadership…it should be the centerpiece of all business cultures that seek to amplify gratitude, purpose, and love."
- **Raki McGregor**: SVP, Novant Health

"If you're looking to engage your teams with a different type of conversation, I encourage you to explore what Glenn Thomas can offer you and your team. My team had great feedback and would like to see him back again! Doing what we've always done may not get us the results we currently need. It's certainly time we do things differently, so thank you, Glenn, for broadening our perspectives in and out of the workplace."
- **Dr. Angela Alston**: Chief Diversity Officer, The Ohio State University College of Nursing

"Glenn Thomas is the heart of leadership…In this age of management, leaders must have a clean mind and be of clear thinking. Glenn Thomas is an authority in helping leaders get there! Heart Work is where it all starts in order to create the necessary follower-ship required to lead successful organizations…His work is cutting-edge and inspiring!"
- **Wendell Davis**: Former Durham County, NC County Manager

This publication is designed to provide accurate and authoritative information in regard to the subject matter covered. It is sold with the understanding that neither the author nor the publisher is engaged in rendering legal, accounting, securities trading, or other professional services. If legal advice or other expert assistance is required, the services of a competent professional person should be sought.

From a Declaration of Principles Jointly Adopted by a Committee of the American Bar Association and a Committee of Publishers and Associations.

This publication was written and edited by the staff team at Heart Work Leadership Group.

Publisher: Heart Work Books & Publishing, LLC, 2021

Paperback ISBN: 978-0-578-24974-2

Heart Work

There is a powerful generosity that exists in our human hearts. The human species is universally connected through a spirit of divine togetherness manifested through *heart work*. Heart Work is the transformative practice of personal vulnerability, honesty, and introspection, as one seeks to live a life of extreme gratitude, intentional purpose, and resilient love. Heart Work influences the way we show up in the world and impacts the people we encounter along the way. It is indeed the most necessary work that we have the privilege to endeavor.

This resource guide was created to expand on the work first highlighted in *Heart Work: 19 Expressions of Heart-centered Leaders*, written by Glenn Thomas, and is a critical and essential resource that adds value to the Heart Work experience. This guide covers the nineteen expressions of *heart-centered leaders* (pay attention to this term) with personal stories and evidence-based research that answers the leadership question: *How do we live, love, and lead from the inside out?*

We created this guide specifically for leaders to uncover how meaningful personal development translates into organizational transformations. Followership is not a by-product of managing people, but it is a result of inspiring, empowering, and leading from a place of *heart-centered* love. We hope this guide adds value to your personal and professional journey in life, love, and leadership. From our hearts to yours - we love you!

About Heart Work Leadership Group

Heart Work Leadership Group, LLC is a leadership development and consultancy firm that focuses on the heart of leadership: *Gratitude, Purpose, and Love.* We have matured intellectually since we started serving leaders in 2013. But the one principle that has never left us is that we believe in the fundamental ideology that leadership begins with loving people.

Numerous research studies inform us that when people feel valued, empowered, and safe, they can achieve the most audacious goals in life. And when they feel loved and cared for, everything is possible.

We cherish the opportunities to work with leaders and organizations seeking to grow themselves through intrapersonal and interpersonal development. Our mantra is simple: "Live to Lead. Lead with Love. Love with Conviction."

We have seen how our principles and strategies position leaders for personal and professional success.   Heart Work Leadership Group continues to develop and curate content and learning experiences that spark inherent greatness.

We started this firm because we wanted to create an organization that *we* wanted to be excited about working for - and we are proud to say we are doing just that; creating a culture that represents all of what we stand for; and educating, empowering, and inspiring organizations and leaders to live better so that they can lead better.

Contents: Expressions of Heart-Centered Leaders

1. Gratitude

Introduction

In any language, few words could be more basic yet meaningful to the human spirit. These words, expressing gratitude and appreciation, can inject any atmosphere, like a shot of B12 with energy, with ideas, creativity, and ingenuity that can't be matched. However, without these simple words, feelings of resentment, envy, and distrust can fester and infect like a viral contagion. The purpose of this lesson is to explore the meaningfulness of gratitude and its impact on life and leadership.

Gratitude is defined as thankfulness or gratefulness, and it comes from the Latin word gratia meaning grace or graciousness. All words derived from this Latin root have to do with kindness, generosity, gifts, the beauty of giving and receiving, or getting something for nothing (DiFabio, et al., 2017).

In marriage, simply saying "Thank you" as a practice can mean the difference between feeling you are in a loving, engaged partnership or being viewed as an entitled taker and user. In parenting, a "Thank you" to a child for a clean room can encourage that child to maintain their space to continue receiving positive reinforcements. In business, an employer who practices gratitude towards their employees has been known to increase productivity, shape morale, strengthen retention, and even minimize the use of sick days within an organization (Mosley, 2019).

Gratitude is the most effective way to cultivate a climate for growth in professional landscapes, and it doesn't require specialized training or equipment to be put to use. Gratitude influences and inspires workers to use their talents and meet objectives head-on as it builds confidence (Mosley, 2019).

Gratitude is reciprocal; the more we are appreciated, the more we understand others. Expressing gratitude is the surest way to show others that their contributions are valued. There is an inherent dignity in hard work. In business, the habit of gratitude affirms that dignity strengthens both the individual and the team. As we explore how the influence of gratitude can positively structure a work environment, think about how you can put this simple act into practice in your professional life.

Gratitude promotes health and productivity

"Acknowledging the good that you already have in your life is the foundation for all abundance." - Eckhart Tolle

With an ever-evolving workplace landscape due to Covid-19 and many employees working remotely, we are all faced with varying personal and professional challenges and distractions (Nawaz et al., 2020). Managing work-life balance has taken on new meaning. Leaders must keep teams focused, engaged, and vested in the business's success by promoting cultures that value employees.

Simply put, gratitude sustains the performance of a workforce because valued employees are happy employees, and happy employees produce results consistently, demonstrating their willingness to help. It is quite a vital task to delegate to a team of appreciated and happy employees (Mosley, 2019). Acknowledging the group's contributions through gratitude also combats toxic emotions within a workforce, such as resentment or indifference about the work that needs to be done (DiFabio, et al., 2017).

Gratitude in business is cost-effective

The Integrated Benefits Institute (IBI), a non-profit health and productivity research organization, reported in November 2018 that "illness-related lost productivity costs US employers $530 billion per year." Thomas Parry, Ph.D., IBI President, states, "To put this in further context, the cost of poor health to employers is greater than the combined revenues of Apple, Amazon, Microsoft, Netflix, eBay, and Adobe" (IBI, 2018).

Painful and unavoidable terminal illness notwithstanding, recognizing the impact that a climate of gratitude creates and that systemically shifts these statistics into a margin of profitability is not an overstatement. Gratitude is scientifically proven to minimize stress, directly reducing the risk of heart disease, cardiovascular disease, increased blood pressure, and strokes (Heubeck et al., 2006). Stress hormones like cortisol are reduced by 23%. This creates resilience in employees when complications do inevitably arise in business.

Gratitude promotes more restful sleep, patience, and a generally peaceful state of mind in employees (Dunn, et al., 2015). Creating an environment of mutual respect and appreciation for the dignity of hard work reduces feelings of worthlessness, depression, and anxiety within the workforce.

Gratitude influences and inspires

Zig Ziglar says, "Gratitude is the highest of all human emotions. The more you express gratitude, the more likely you will have even more to express gratitude for."

Dr. Robert A. Emmons, Ph.D., the world's leading scientific expert on gratitude, professor of psychology at the University of California at Davis, and the founding editor-in-chief of The Journal of Positive Psychology believes that gratitude has two main components: (1) the affirmation of goodness; identifying goodness in our own lives, and (2) knowing that goodness originates outside of ourselves, which encourages humility (DiFabio, et al., 2017). When we are in the habit of showing gratitude, we acknowledge that it is the contributions of others that have helped us achieve goodness in our lives - and conversely, that we can contribute to the goodness in the lives of others. As it is said, no man is an island.

In the work environment, this meaningfulness of work satisfies a deep human need to be helpful, be a part of the whole, and demonstrate our merit through achieving a common goal (Mosley, 2019). It fosters camaraderie and transparency within a group, a team, or a department. Recognizing each individual's contribution creates *psychological safety*, wherein workers feel comfortable asking for help, knowing they won't be penalized or belittled for it (DiFabio, et al., 2017). It even transforms past challenges and disappointments into opportunities for growth and advancement.

This ability to positively impact the trajectory of an organization from a leadership perspective, all by simply saying, "Thank you, your point of view is so valuable," is incredibly powerful. The sustainable benefits of gratitude can take time, but they have a far-reaching influence once established. Gratitude is best shown as culture, not just moment-by-moment pep talks. So often, much of our time and energy is spent pursuing things we currently don't have. The gratitude level sets what matters most and helps us appreciate all that exists.

Exercise

The year 2020 presented more than ample opportunities to complain and to forget to express gratitude-between the pandemic, social unrest, political divisiveness, economic challenges, to mask or not to mask, the toilet tissue dilemma, you name it.

Nevertheless, there have also been countless opportunities to express gratitude; from retired teachers choosing to tutor students for free over Zoom, to healthcare workers battling the pandemic on the frontlines for all of our well-being, to neighbors spontaneously paying for the groceries of hundreds of shoppers, human kindness and dignity still exist.

For the last 15-20 minutes of this lesson, write a statement of gratitude to an essential worker. Being "essential" is often a thankless role with minimal pay and benefits. Yet many show up for all of us every day with gratitude. These essential workers let their hard work speak for itself. For this exercise, choose one essential worker, whether or not you know their name; the gas station attendant, the server or bartender, the retail associate, the truck driver, the first responder, postal worker, health care worker, or teacher. Write out a statement of gratitude as if you're speaking to them. Thank them. Express the impact they've had on you. Place yourself in their shoes and share the sentiments that you want them to hear.

Once done, write a second statement of how it would feel to be able to read those words to that person who may have never known how they influenced you or that they were even visible to you. How does it feel telling someone they are seen and appreciated? Hopefully, you will find that this attitude of gratitude will have rippling effects on how you view and contribute to the world going forward. *By the way, you can share your letter too… which may just make their day!*

2. Purpose

Introduction

Several years ago, Rick Warren's *A Purpose Driven Life* reignited a discussion that has been the topic of philosophical, religious, and ideological debates, perhaps since the first man became a living soul. Warren's book appeared on the New York Times best-seller list for over ninety weeks in 2008 and remained one of the top-selling non-fiction books in history, selling thirty-two million copies within its first decade. The introspective, self-reflective questions remain with many: "Why are we here?" More to the point, "Why am I here? What is my purpose? And "How do I live a life of purpose?" For most, the fundamental premise of the question certainly feels like one that should be answered quickly.

And once *purpose* is discovered, honing those innate gifts and talents and developing them into skills and careers also seems like it should be an eventuality. Yet, very few of us do the work needed to reveal what's been right under our proverbial noses. Whether it was an interest in taking your favorite toys or gadgets apart to understand how they worked as a child or being the trusted friend in college whom all your other friends came to when they had a big decision to make; *purpose* is often hidden among the uneventful, often mundane details of our daily existence. Usually, it takes a good teacher, a coach, or a leader - people in leadership positions whose job is to develop and craft individual talent - to help us recognize what has been there all along.

But not all leadership is created equal. It takes a thoughtful leader to recognize those "diamond-in-the-rough" talents and develop them into meaningful and purposeful contributors. On the contrary, when individual *purpose* is a non-factor, projects suffer, teams lose morale, and results are mediocre.

So, how does leadership transition from merely overseeing teams and departments into fully utilizing the unique workforce they're responsible for? How does *leadership* influence its workforce to move from having a purpose to *purpose* having an impact?

Purpose-driven leadership

Academics argue persuasively that an executive's most important role is to be a steward of an organization's purpose. Business experts make the case that purpose is a key to exceptional performance, while psychologists describe it as the pathway to greater well-being. Despite the clear benefits of discovering one's purpose, fewer than 20% of leaders say they have a strong sense of *purpose*. Even fewer can summarize their *purpose* in one concrete, individualized statement. And even more discouraging, hardly any persons in leadership have a clear plan for themselves to translate that purpose into action. Most have simply decided to forgo the existential question altogether. The result is an existence of limited aspirations and often a failure to achieve their most ambitious professional and personal goals (Craig and Snook, 2014).

A leader's personal reflection: *Before 2020, it had been easy for me to simply phone into my own life, both professionally and personally. I was a human resources manager for a central manufacturing plant for eight years. At the time, I would have said I enjoyed my career and my work. I viewed my position as a type of guide, assisting my team through education and organizational means so that they could be vital contributors to the success of our company. I encouraged my workforce always to remain teachable and seek opportunities to learn multiple jobs within the plant. My crew was happy and felt heard. Executive management was satisfied as I was both reliable and effective. I met challenges head-on. I took ownership of the needs of my workforce, and I readily addressed those needs with thoroughness and compassion. I received many commendations over the years for my commitment and consistent results.*

However, as a Leader, I was incredibly unfulfilled. Fulfillment, frankly, seemed like an ideal that was above my pay grade. I'd repeat the performance day in and day out. Weeks turned to years so quickly. And before I knew it, nearly a decade had passed, and I had no idea why I was even there.

- *What is my purpose in this career?*
- *What am I contributing here in a way that no one else can?*
- *Aside from the obvious benefits of having an income, why am I in this particular career?*
- *In what way has this career fulfilled me?*

For many like me, it took a pandemic and a worldwide economic crisis of biblical proportion to prompt some serious self-reflection. When the whole world shut down, and there was nothing but time to reflect, most were forced to take a hard look at the question of who they were. And how would they navigate whom they were toward reconstructing a new normal, safe and productive life for themselves and their families? I, for one, learned that I am, at my core, an educator. Teachable moments energize me, and I like the challenge of taking messy, unfavorable circumstances and making them turning points for others to grow. I am fulfilled when I can lead others to grow and expand. As leaders in our professional and personal lives, answering the questions of purpose has quickly become paramount to surviving and thriving. The most important developmental task you can undertake as a leader is articulating your purpose and finding the courage to live it.

In leadership, it is vital that you mine your story for those significant themes in life that reveal your lifelong passions and values. Look for a common thread throughout your life and note the times, places, and events that energized you. Again, often our purpose lies quietly and unremarkably in the most mundane details. It may seem mundane, but it is exceptional and impressive to others. Once you've recognized those major themes from your life, you must craft a concise and personal purpose statement; something that gets you motivated. Then finally, it is vital that you establish a "Purpose-to-Impact" plan. Focus on big aspirations, broken down into shorter-term goals. Then "work backward," taking small achievable steps with increasing specificity (Craig and Snook, 2014).

Visionary leadership

Fundamentally, leaders must have a plan and a direction in which they lead. Being intentional about decision-making gains the confidence and commitment of others to your vision for the collective. And when you have considered everyone's passions and values, the dynamic you've created is one of cohesion and a new shared vision. Creating a shared vision takes experience as a leader; no one is born knowing how to navigate multiple personalities. It takes time. It takes intention. It takes communication.

Quality communication about goals means sharing your road map and connecting it to the organization's larger vision. Leaders must express a clear and achievable future to orient everyone toward it. Then ensure that employees know their contributions are vital to achieving that future. Their work must be recognized as meaningful if they are to follow you. This boosts morale and supports an attitude that each team member is precisely where they need to be, doing exactly what they should be doing. Knowing you are a part of a shared vision and shared purpose emboldens creativity and increases job satisfaction (Hedges, 2018).

Conversely, it must be noted that to ignore purpose as a critical component in successful leadership is to choose not to be a leader with intent and purpose behind their motives; you may easily fall into one of several less favorable categories of leaders: panic leadership, denialist leadership, or just plain incompetent leadership (Tourish, 2020).

Leaders produce leaders

"True leaders don't create followers. True leaders create more leaders."

Not all leaders lead with purpose. Some simply lead with a stated objective and a mandate to their team to meet that objective within a said time frame. However, to lead with purpose is to be an exceptional leader. Being an excellent leader means getting extraordinary achievements from everyday people. Among the most memorable achievements of outstanding, purposeful leadership is the ability to illuminate one's abilities.

When leaders lead with a mission and a bright vision for the future, it encourages their team to see the possibilities of their purpose. Team members learn to mine their own stories to find the thing(s) that make them unique, the qualities that are missed when they are not present. They learn to become subject-matter experts and good stewards of their respective expertise to the larger vision. These growing leaders seek opportunities to make things work better and more efficiently together. They want to be relied upon because that means their contributions are meaningful. A sense of community and shared experiences is fostered. Their knowledge and understanding of organization expand, and they, in turn, find their place in their career and life. The place they were always meant to be was waiting for them all along. Isn't that the purpose of *purposeful leadership,* after all?

Exercise

What is the thing that makes you "tick?" What experiences consistently excite you? Ask 2-3 people you've known the longest (parents, siblings, former teachers/coaches, or best friends); what would they miss if you were not around?

From your research and reflection, write a clear and concise purpose statement; nothing canned. Make it meaningful to you – even if it means nothing to anyone else. Make sure that it energizes and motivates you. Next, make a plan to fulfill your purpose. Write it out. Set a big goal where your objective is most passionately fulfilled within three years. Then set slightly smaller but achievable goals within one year. Then set smaller goals achievable within six months, 90 days, and two weeks.

3. Love

Introduction

What is a 4-letter word most employers refuse to say out loud because they view it as an inappropriate language for the workplace? Most employees and their managers steer clear of this language for fear of igniting a human resources investigation of inappropriate workplace behavior. It may not be the word you're thinking.

The word is LOVE.

Not "love" as in, "I love my morning coffee," or "I love the view from my new office,"… but LOVE, as in "I love my team," or "I love and respect my boss" or, "I love and trust my colleagues."

Love is a central focus as it relates to the people, not just peripheral details of the work environment; love as it relates to the people who make an organization what it is; love from leadership that impacts the diverse layers of an organization: real, actual LOVE.

Is this making you uncomfortable? Despite the understandably uneasy feeling of mixing such an emotion-filled word with the work environment, the truth is that the concept is not so unorthodox.   Love is the single most driving force in human existence. Nothing motivates or inspires like love. Nothing pushes us out of our comfort zone and sparks creative expressions like love.

So why do so many in leadership tip-toe around the subject so awkwardly? Why don't more leaders harness this basic need of human existence to pull the best out of people? We have collectively agreed that this universal "good" is somehow not appropriate in the place where we spend most of our waking hours (Coombe, 2016).

How much more would an organization flourish and grow if, first, the people flourished in a professional sphere where they felt supported, respected, valued, and loved?

Unfortunately, western culture takes a minimal 1-or 2-dimensional interpretation of the word. This view is the essence of the discomfort for many if the subject is breached in the workplace. Instead, the topic is avoided altogether. Of course, romantic and physical love is inappropriate and counterproductive to the goals of any organization – that is without question. Yet, consider the ancient Greeks, who understood that romantic love is only one kind of love.

These scholars, philosophers, and profound thinkers of math, science, and the cosmos, also recognized that love has dimensions and differing manifestations. They perceived that love exists on a spectrum and that there could be only one kind of love was simply preposterous. They formulated several different words to provide context when the subject inevitably arose.

There's AGAPE, considered the highest form of the word, emphasizing purity, selflessness, and the unconditional nature of the emotion. AGAPE is the word at the heart of the Judeo-Christian definition of God's love as defined in 1 Corinthians 13. "Love is patient and kind… it doesn't boast, it doesn't keep a record of wrongs…love never fails." AGAPE is an exacting and perfect supernatural love. Then there's

PRAGMA, or longstanding love like many of our grandparents and great-grandparents had. This love is steeped in commitment and "sticks it out" for the long haul. There's LUDUS, or what some may recognize as a youthful crush or "puppy" love. Of course, there's EROS, or romantic, sensual love, for the adults in the room; and PHAULITIA, or self-love, simply classified as self-care or self-esteem.

Finally, there's PHILIA, or profound (platonic) friendship, emphasizing trust, virtue, and loyalty. As in Philadelphia or the city of brotherly love, this manifestation denotes trust, camaraderie, empathy, and shared responsibility.

When I speak of the mutual recognition and appreciation that could - and I submit, should exist in all organizations, this is the love I am speaking of. So what role does PHILIA's love play in the workplace? How can leaders adopt an attitude of Philia that will strengthen their organization? Can a culture of unity and shared vision be accomplished without Philia?

The Love Connection

First, it should be recognized that leading a team is a natural outgrowth of loving them. To lead a team, a good leader invests time learning about the individuals who make up their team. Knowing your people and emphasizing their strengths while developing them in the areas where they are weakest is an act of love or Philia. And it requires intention.

When Lieutenant Colonel Joe Ricciardi stood before his battalion of 1000 soldiers deployed to clear roads of improvised explosive devices (IEDs) in Afghanistan, he gave them a straightforward message: "You need to love one another." Despite the initial blank stares he received, Ricciardi went on to define the concept in a way that, before he was done speaking, the battalion responded with clear understanding and acceptance. Love isn't optional when leading or being a part of a team. It's an order! Upon further research into the question of love, as it relates to leadership, Ricciardi concluded that three love factors – intimacy, passion, and commitment – correlated directly with leadership.

Establishing an appropriate and authentic level of intimate knowledge of your team members and exhibiting care about their personal lives generates a bond and demonstrates commitment.   Expressing positive, often contagious energy and passion for your organization's vision and objectives means accomplishing your goals and communicating in a way that compels everyone to meet and exceed their goals.   And again, committing to the development of team members by investing time and effort empowers those individuals to take on more significant, more complex tasks and strengthens their engagement with the larger vision of an organization. "Strong leaders," Ricciardi says, "can also tie your task to a higher purpose, showing how your work influences the greater whole."

These key characteristics tie the concept of love to effective, dynamic leadership.   A team member who feels loved, who is seen, valued, and trusted by their leader is, significantly, more likely to see them as a leader they will follow (Johnson, 2014).

What's Love Got to Do With It?

"Love and Work. Work and Love. That's all there is." - Sigmund Freud

Leading with love takes great courage for all the reasons mentioned above. On the surface, it's a radical concept that contradicts what most people have ever been taught about business. Love is still a very complex and not easily defined word. But herein lies the beauty: Love doesn't have to be openly defined or even called "love" to impact and shape an organization. The idea is to express concern and care for the welfare, growth, and wholeness of others, whether that manifests as compassion, respect, or simple small kindnesses. It doesn't require awkward discussion or deliberation. Some of the most heart-centered corporate executives say they let their company's actions, policies, products, and services speak love for them.

Love in leadership and within an organization should act as a behind-the-scenes operating system that supports the functional elements of business, like human resources, finance, sales, etc. As anyone in the IT profession would tell you, when you have a great operating system, all other applications work smoothly and cohesively. That's the role that love-led leadership should play. It should also be noted that loving leadership doesn't mean that every day is intended to be a bed of roses in an organization. So-called "tough love" certainly has its place when leading a team. Love in the workplace is about being comfortable with conflict, difficult conversations and expressly encouraging self-accountability while remaining mindful of their dignities.

Another critical factor to consider is that love does need to be invited into an organization. Like radio waves, love is always present. We just need to tune into its frequency. As stated previously, love is a fundamental need in human existence. Therefore, love exists wherever people exist. Whether a welcoming smile from your boss in the morning, a kind word from a colleague, or concern when a co-worker is struggling, love is at work in all of these instances, even when unspoken. When love is considered a worthwhile pursuit in any aspect of business or life, both leaders and team members have the opportunity to express love throughout their lives, including at work (Coombe, 2016).

The Servant-Leader

Many scholars draw from the perspective that the nature of the leader-follower relationship is enshrined in a sacred and moral obligation and dedication to their followers' best interests. This stewardship theory illustrates love as a servant-leader. In service to others, leaders can fully develop their team and organization to achieve their highest potential.   Being a servant-leader means having the capacity to see the value of each individual's contribution and to use it for the greater good.   This is love demonstrated through relationship and humility.   Leaders must be willing to give of themselves to help others achieve their highest potential and create a better organization.

Loving self is seeking to improve oneself to serve others better. In addition, love is always seeking out the best in people. Treating employees as valued partners in decision-making and profit sharing demonstrates trust.   Trust is foundational to any human connection, whether professional or personal.   A servant-leader focuses on and invests time in the development of the team to trust them with greater responsibilities and the opportunity for greater rewards. Many companies who have adopted *high-performance work systems* that treat employees as valued partners have consistently been found to be more profitable than peer competitors who do not treat employees with care.

Further, employees of these companies who have maintained an "arms-length" relationship frequently express distrust in their leadership, a general lack of commitment to the company's growth and vision, and dissatisfaction with little professional development efforts. This *leadership* doesn't care; consequently, their employees don't either. In a global workforce, where 71% of employees are actively looking for new jobs, the importance of creating better relationships between leaders and followers seems to be a no-brainer.

Evidence suggests that love's capacity to bring out the best in individuals is exemplified by high trust and individual commitment. Bringing out the best in your employees creates wealth and adds value to organizations and their employees. Organizations that adopt this highly humanistic approach encourage the hearts of their employees. Employees know they are valued. They understand they are not just laborers or means of production. Applying the principle of love, as in Philia, to a leader's relationship with employees in a work context makes excellent business sense. It arms the importance of love and trust as aligned leadership virtues (Anderson et al., 2019).

Exercise

Imagine you are a department manager for an advertising firm. *Angela* has been an entry-level graphic designer with the company for two years. She's expressed interest in leading the graphic design team on a new campaign. And she usually demonstrates excellent organizational and creative design skills, but she recently missed a critical deadline. Angela is also a recent divorcee amid a financially straining custody battle. She's also had to move her sick, elderly father into her home to care for him.

Create an action plan for how to support and develop Angela in reaching her professional and personal goals. Is she ready for the promotion? How do you communicate whether or not she's prepared for a leadership position? How do you demonstrate love for Angela, considering all of the circumstances?

4. Joy

Introduction

The world is moving at breakneck speed these days. Everything is urgent. Everything is immediate. Everything needs our attention yesterday. People are burning the candle at both ends just to keep up. The race to acquire things is endless. The competition to be the first or the best or the only is a spinning, revolving door of short-lived victories. Very few people commit time and energy just to take it all in. Very little time is set aside even to process, let alone to savor or enjoy the fruits of their labor.

Yet, in business, we appear taken aback by the burn-out and mental and emotional breakdowns occurring among our deeply strained workforce. It can ultimately be counterproductive to push ourselves so hard for so long because, in the end, despite all efforts to the contrary, many need mental health days and even sick days to recuperate from the pace of it all.

So why are we doing this to ourselves? As leaders, why are we doing this to our teams? How much more would we benefit in life and business if we allowed ourselves to simplify our thinking and recognize the joy in the ordinary again? At the risk of sounding cliche, there's so much more to our lives than the things we possess or even the things we accomplish. Those possessions and accomplishments mean so little if our families, spouses, and children can never experience us with a full tank. Ironically, choosing a joyful attitude makes us better suited for the challenges we face and the work that needs to be done.

Studies have shown that happy people are more substantial, more productive assets to any organization (Zwilling, et al., 2016). They are great collaborators because, as happier people, they are far less stressed and nicer to work with. Their disposition lends to more creativity, more innovative ideas, and more problem solving, which builds both self-confidence and the confidence of others in their adeptness in their role (Zwilling, et al., 2016). The list of benefits goes on.

As leaders, it is essential, for long-term success, that we encourage balance for ourselves and our teams. When we adopt a joyful, positive attitude, we set a healthy example for our teams.

The Simple Things

Developing a joyful, positive attitude can seem almost too simple; we often over-complicate the concept. Focusing on positivity by making small, minor adjustments to our attitude can have far-reaching ripple effects on our daily lives. Creating a morning routine, for example, can be highly effective (Fabrega). Setting aside time for self-care, like taking a quiet 20-minute walk or practicing meditation as a part of your morning routine, might seem like a trivial thing that can be skipped. But the truth is, in small but impactful doses, consistent self-care can be just as important as eating breakfast. We must fuel both our bodies as well as our minds when preparing for the day ahead.

Also, instead of turning on the news or CNBC's stock reports first thing in the morning, try starting the day by listening to positive affirmations or upbeat music with a positive message for a few minutes. Condition your mind by feeding it good energy before the day's stress even gets the chance to set in.

Regularly beginning your day with "joyful noise," instead of the incessant racket of the world around us, keeps us grounded.

Another valuable but often overlooked behavior in leadership is the simple act of smiling. Many leaders in varying organizations have wrongly assumed that to be taken seriously as a leader, you must always be serious (Zwilling et al., 2016). Not so. Again, it's about balance. Scientists say that when we smile, our brains release tiny molecules called neuropeptides that help fight off stress. This release of neuropeptides sets off a chain reaction of neurotransmitters like serotonin and endorphins, which act as nature's pain relievers and anti-depressants.

Research shows that teams under the leadership of men and women who rarely laugh or smile are generally dissatisfied with their position, even if they are ideally suited for the role in skill and experience. They feel uncertain about their future with the company, and many harbor a general distrust of colleagues and their managers. On the contrary, a manager with a more positive disposition and who smiles often is viewed as trustworthy and supportive. Team members under this kind of leader describe their work environment as bolstering, engaging, and fun (Zwilling, et al., 2016). These employees were also more likely to find their work rewarding and less afraid to ask for help (Zwilling, et al., 2016).

It's incredible how a simple smile from a leader can be essential in reversing negative and inefficient energy. (Fabrega). Leaders must know that smiling is not only okay but can also be instrumental in getting optimal results from your team.

BYOJ ("Bring Your Own Joy")

Joy cannot be forced, but we train our brains to choose joy when we practice a positive attitude.   Yes, joy, like most human emotions, is a choice. It requires a conscious and deliberate act of focus, dedication, and perseverance.   Joy is not just moments of happiness; choosing joy doesn't mean every moment is joyful or ignoring the less-than-joyful experiences.   On the contrary, joy acts like rain gear amid the storm.

And choosing joy doesn't just make us happier; it makes us more resilient (Fabrega). Joy is about wholeness. When we exercise our emotional muscles to choose joy in the face of adversity or failure, we choose strength. Perseverance is essential in all facets of business and life. Joy is how we persevere. By exercising gratitude, embracing the lessons learned, and practicing patience and grace with ourselves, we can maintain a joyful attitude through difficulties and elevate our emotional intelligence in ways that can't be matched by life's more leisurely days (Fabrega).

The Joys of Leadership

A leader assigned to guide and develop a team of employees is an extraordinary responsibility. Setting the example of joy and positivity and establishing a tone of resilience within an organization is undoubtedly easier said than done. But it is possible, and even more so, hugely beneficial. When employees experience their leaders taking responsibility for their attitude, especially when faced with challenges, they see the value in taking charge of their behavior and attitudes in their own lives.

They see that they are not victims of circumstance but strong, confident, capable individuals who can choose to control the controllable and withstand the challenges that are out of their control. Team members need to see their leaders be human and imperfect from time to time; it's relatable. However, they do not need to see their leaders broken, bitter, and overtaken by those imperfect moments. Joy is how healthy leaders keep the ship steady and press forward to sail another day.

Exercise

Name a song, a book, a proverb, or a poem that makes you smile and can jump-start your day or break you out of an emotional funk when necessary. What key lyric or phrase speaks directly to what you need to hear in those difficult times?

Make your mission statement, using this key phrase or lyric as inspiration. Make it personal. For example, "I have the serenity to accept the things I cannot change. I am courageous and will change the things I can. I am wise enough to know the difference." Share your mission statement with others, and be amazed by what happens.

5. Heart Intelligence

Introduction

Heart intelligence is the flow of consciousness, understanding, and intuition we experience when the mind and emotions are brought into coherent alignment with the heart (Heart Intelligence, 2012).

It's no coincidence that the heart was viewed as the primary source of virtue and intelligence in ancient Greece and China. Many faith traditions refer to the heart as the seat of the soul (The Heart - An Agent of Transformation, 2015).

In western cultures, however, we have been taught that intelligence (the ability to learn, understand, reason, and apply knowledge) originates in the brain (Heart Intelligence, 2012), and the heart manages emotion and feelings. It was only recently, in the 1990s, that neuro-cardiologists discovered that the heart-brain has neurons that can sense, feel, learn and remember, then send this information in the form of a heart rhythm pattern to the amygdala, thalamus, and frontal lobes.

It is the heart that is the most intelligent and most fascinating aspect of our existence. It is our heart that does the heavy lifting. The functions and experiences we attribute to our brains have originated in our hearts.

The heart can be exercised through deliberate practice, and the more we pay attention when we sense the heart is speaking to us or guiding us, the greater our ability to access its intelligence and guidance. Neuro-cardiologists have discovered that heart intelligence supports cellular organization and guides and grows organisms toward balance, awareness, and coherence of their bodies systems. Simply put, it is our heart that pilots the plane! The health and balance of the heart affect the entire body on a cellular level.

Developing Heart Intelligence

Heart intelligence is developed and enhanced by paying attention to the world and one's place in it. It requires a heightened sense of internal and external awareness. Leaders tend to be focused on intellectual concepts, using their brains to solve problems and make decisions. But thinking also happens in the heart, and most leaders know what it feels like to have "a gut feeling."

For example, the act of leadership and the commitment it requires is not something that can be fully understood on an intellectual level. Leadership is a calling (of nature and nurture), and the calling happens in our "gut" or the heart. Explaining how it happens can be difficult to describe. But "trusting our gut" is just as accurate as any other thought. Being called to leadership generates a sense of purpose that drives leaders in ways that go beyond status, recognition, or financial compensation. It is a feeling that informs everything leaders do and is an indicator of a person who has developed heart intelligence.

Leading with an Intelligent Heart

In business, when leaders learn and apply this vital information about how their employees are wired and understand the fundamental role the heart plays, it informs how they lead and makes them more intuitive communicators and leaders.

Applying heart intelligence in leadership roles means learning new ways of communicating that open up the hearts and minds of your teams to new insights. Leading with heart intelligence means developing communication strategies and tools to create healthy workplaces. By learning heart intelligence as a leader, you can generate higher levels of intuition about your team by seeing patterns that lead to more significant insights. It is so exciting that more and more people intuitively sense the importance of including the heart in our interactions. They recognize that the heart's input is essential for making wiser decisions. Some have called this emotional intelligence, but it's heart intelligence (Glaser, et al., 2016). Listening to our hearts as leaders makes for wiser, more adept leaders.

> *"Researchers have concluded that intelligence and intuition are heightened when we learn to listen more deeply to our own heart. Learning how to decipher messages, we receive from our heart gives us the keen perception needed to manage our emotions amid life's challenges effectively. Without the guiding influence of*

the heart, we are more likely to react with pointless emotions such as insecurity, anger, fear, blame, and other energy-draining reactions and behaviors. The more we learn to listen to and follow our heart intelligence, the more educated, balanced, and coherent our emotions become (Glaser, et al., 2016).

Heart & Conversation Intelligence

Conversational intelligence addresses the "alchemy of trust" in the heart during our conversations. You could think of heart rhythm as the physical manifestation of that chemical reaction. When we engage with someone and feel trust or distrust, our hearts will show the essence of how we are connecting with that person. When we trust, our heart rhythm is steady, and we can hear; without any obstruction, the message is being conveyed. We trust the message because we trust the messenger. However, when we feel distrust, the opposite is true. Our heart speaks up, and our heart rhythm increases, sending signals to the rest of our body. We might call this intuition.

Trust makes all the difference because it begins and ends in our hearts. Conversational intelligence distinguishes three levels of conversation that help define how we converse with others. Each level has a purpose:

- Level I Conversations are not deep, not outside of what people already know.

- Level II Conversations are negotiations where people hold onto their viewpoints. These conversations follow a very familiar pattern: we advocate our point of view and inquire about others' points of view – in the spirit of influencing others to adopt our line of thinking.

- Level III Conversations are where people's prefrontal cortex/ heart connection becomes accessible to them, creating a secure environment where people are more comfortable opening up; where you can pick up the energetic field of others more clearly, and intuitively sense the appropriate response (Glaser, et al., 2016).

Heart intelligence is transformational to how leaders communicate, shape, and develop their employees. As it becomes more commonly recognized as revolutionary thinking, more leaders will become more balanced and set the example of heart intelligence and balance for their teams and their organizations.

Exercise

Practice using your senses, including your heart: Practice experiencing life more through your heart. You can see much more when you see with your heart. Hear, taste, touch, and feel life with your heart. There is thinking about your experience, and there is being very present and feeling your experience with your heart. How is life different when your heart is included? What do you learn about yourself that you otherwise would not have if you had not taken time with your heart?

Reference: Bruce Davis, Ph.D. https://www.huffpost.com/entry/school-days-again-ten-exe_b_5600857

6. Resilience

Introduction

In the 2006 movie *Rocky Balboa*, Rocky is confronted by his son, who feels he's been slighted his whole life by having to live in his father's shadow. He refers to the perks, but more so, the pressures of the Balboa name. In response, Rocky makes what is arguably one of the sincerest, most inspirational, most heartfelt speeches ever documented on screen. For me, the script frankly leaped from the big screen and into my storyline in a way that compelled some pretty deep self-reflection for days after:

> *"Let me tell you something you already know. The world ain't all sunshine and rainbows. It's a very*

mean and nasty place, and I don't care how tough you are; it will beat you to your knees and keep you there permanently if you let it. You, me, or nobody is gonna hit as hard as life. But it ain't about how hard ya hit. It's about how hard you can get hit and keep moving forward. How much you can take and keep moving forward. That's how winning is done!"

"Now if you know what you're worth then go out and get what you're worth. But you gotta be willing to take the hits, and not pointing fingers saying you ain't where you wanna be because of him, or her, or anybody! Cowards do that and that ain't you! You're better than that! I'm always gonna love you no matter what. No matter what happens. You're my son and you're my blood. You're the best thing in my life. But until you start believing in yourself, ya ain't gonna have a life (Stallone, 2006)."

How winning is done

The philosophy is that you've already lost when entering any "ring" in life, whether personally or professionally, with even a fraction of self-defeating thinking and destructive self-talk. Whatever the arena, whatever the "fight," winning begins and ends within you, first. And there's no room for bitterness or blaming others - it's you! Before facing any challenge, we must first win the battle against our self-doubt and defeatist attitudes. And if that's not the fight you're willing to take on, well then, you'll never truly live or achieve the things you want out of life.

A powerful and dynamic lesson from a father to a son, from director to movie audiences, from leader to team. The perspective is applicable and wide-ranging, both galvanizing and disillusioning. It is a lesson that shatters the son's naivety that the world should be fair and just. In reality, there is no such world. In leadership, conditioning the minds of your team to recognize that the win is within the adversity is foundational to developing a high-performing team. Getting stuck in it is not an option when challenges are anticipated and mentally prepared for. You must get up. You must move forward! Resilience is the power that fuels our becoming.

Resilience, of course, can be defined in many ways. Still, it all boils down to the human capacity to meet adversity, setbacks, and trauma and recover as a better, wiser, stronger person. It is the capacity not only to endure struggle or hardship but to grow in the midst of it. Resilient leaders can sustain their energy level under pressure, cope with disruptive changes, and adapt. They bounce back from setbacks. They also overcome significant difficulties without engaging in dysfunctional behavior or harming others (Kohlrieser, 2015).

But what is the essence of resilience? Where does it come from? Is it a quality, a skill, or a personality trait? Is it genetically determined, or can it be taught? Expert discussion is ongoing, but current thinking is clear: resilience can be developed and improved. Experts assert that resilience is a quality and a skill that can be enhanced yet requires "effort and consistency" (Doll, 2021).

Being A Resilient Leader

Resilient leaders cultivate high-performing teams through self-leadership first. Leaders must be driven to grow (or enhance) their ability to adapt and recover from personal and professional setbacks. It is often forgotten that one must learn to lead oneself before being able to teach others successfully. Leaders must cultivate resilience in themselves to advance and thrive.

How well leaders cope with stress helps determine how resilient they are overall and how effective they can be at coaching resilience to their teams through stressful situations. Studies have shown that stress is not, in and of itself harmful. Chronic worry is destructive. But stress reactions, such as a pounding heart and fast breathing, prepare our bodies to meet a threat. They energize us to act. Leaders should experience a sense of urgency when deadlines are fast approaching, it's "crunch time," and their projects are at stake. Momentary stress can help motivate individuals and teams at a critical juncture. However, a resilient leader knows to temper momentary stress by remaining grounded and maintaining a balanced perspective. Such leaders recognize that obtaining results is essential, but getting overly stressed – or stressing their team does not increase effectiveness or productivity. The balanced approach to stress is the ability to return to a positive mental state as quickly as reasonably possible.

To enhance their resilience, leaders should identify the coping mechanisms that allow them to relieve tension and regain positive energy. These stress management tools include being aware of stress responses, talking out worries and concerns, creating specific goals by prioritizing, and knowing when it's time to grieve and when it's time to let go of a loss. It is also essential for leaders to practice self-care by eating healthy and committing to getting a whole night's rest regularly. The ability to work through adversity is null and void if you're only operating on half a tank.

Resilient leaders know that life isn't about floating through the world on a breeze or skating by all of life's many challenges unscathed. Instead, it's about experiencing the losses and all the negative, complex, and distressing events that life throws at you while staying on task and remaining optimistic and high-functioning. Developing resilience requires emotional distress. If we never ran into disappointment in the first place, we would never learn how to deal with it (Kohlrieser, 2015). Resilient leaders adapt and choose to use challenges to strengthen their team and build confidence - first in their leadership, and eventually develop their team members' characters.

Coaching A Resilient Team

High-performing leaders know they have a moral and social obligation to build a team that can persevere through adversity. They must duplicate their resilience in others by teaching them how to identify problem areas and create solution strategies. The perspective gained must affirm the employee's capability to meet the challenge, and the coach/ leader must encourage positive self-talk.

Experts have learned that positive self-talk is among the most valuable skills and is also commonly used in the coaching context. Positive self-talk can be taught in the workplace and used as a preventative intervention. These methods are standard practice in workplace coaching, so team members who may require guidance in this area can receive it without feeling singled out. Personal coaching offers the opportunity for confidential and private discussions that may be more conducive to open discussion about difficulties individual team members may be having. Issues that might require working in the resilience domain may be more likely to surface during these private discussions – whether in their personal and professional lives or both (Smith, 2015).

Leaders must be tuned in to the team they have assembled and learn to recognize when a colleague is under much stress. Does the person communicate a lack of meaning in their work? Do they exhibit negativity, over-victimization, or excessive anger? Social behaviors such as lateness and failure to attend meetings are also clues. Often, the best way to initiate the conversation is to ask, "Is everything all right? It appears you may be under much stress. Is there anything I can do to help you?" The questions should be gentle and respectful (Kohlrieser, 2015).

Resilience coaching is often delivered on a proactive basis to enhance skills. Routine resilience coaching, in this context, is intended to strengthen employee confidence and the belief in one's capacity to execute behaviors necessary to produce specific performance results before issues arise. Experts find this proactive approach is more effective than reducing risk factors such as anxiety (Lee, et al., 2013).

Managers have a clear interest in working with vibrant and energetic employees. Stress robs creativity and ingenuity. To avoid stress becoming a performance issue, leaders should actively promote resilience and boost energy in their teams (Kohlrieser, 2015).

Cultivating a positive mindset in team members is key to coaching resilience. Though our brain's natural tendency is to identify threats, we can consciously choose to strengthen specific thought patterns over others. It is as if we had a flashlight in our minds that we could shine in different directions. Our natural tendency is to use this flashlight to look for danger and pain. However, we can train our mind's eyes to refocus. In essence, positive and negative mindsets are malleable (Kohlrieser, 2015).

Resilient leaders have also demonstrated a healthy and balanced sense of humor. They understand that they carry the responsibility for helping to protect the energy of the people on their teams. Much can be gained from leaders who simply seek out opportunities to laugh with their team regularly. Resilience is a deliberate choice. Choosing to laugh is the ultimate symbol of resilience. Heart-centered leaders know that by developing resilient, high-energy, high-functioning employees, they maximize their effectiveness as leaders.

Resilient Leadership Through Crisis

Becoming a leader who can successfully navigate an extraordinarily unpredictable world is more important than ever.   No industry is invulnerable.   From Covid-19 to quarantining and social distancing, to dealing with personal losses of family members and friends, to political and social unrest prompting interpersonal tensions, to protests and riots, to remote learning for school-age children, to choose whether to vaccinate or not to vaccinate – the day to day uncertainties require levels of resilience and coping that take on new meaning in this new, ever-changing world. Companies and industries have been forced to rethink entire organizational structures almost overnight. Leaders have had to learn to manage teams remotely and remain effective, and businesses that have been unable to adapt have been forced to shut their doors (Gavin, 2019).

Leaders must exhibit remarkable self-awareness and emotional intelligence within this heightened landscape of unpredictability in the workplace. As mentioned previously, leaders must regularly take an honest inventory of their wellness before broaching the subject of managing others successfully. Reliance on trusted peers, friends, and colleagues for guidance and strength is critical. Share your concerns and ask questions. Many of your peers may share those concerns. When issues and areas of concern are raised, dialogue can begin, and ideas and strategies to overcome those concerns can be established.

Resilient leaders never stop learning and growing in the area of resilience. When they are open to learning more, it bolsters their resolve to overcome hardships. Emboldened by the support of their peers and equipped with new strategies for success, a resilient leader can adapt their leadership style to tackle these new complexities and more effectively manage their team.

Resilient leaders will reassure their team of their ongoing support and continued belief that the team can meet these new challenges. They will reaffirm each employee's vital role in the team's overall goals and rally the team toward shared objectives. Resilient leadership presses forward, gaining new perspectives and becoming more robust, wiser, and better leaders.

Exercise

Laughter has been found to boost resilience. A study evaluating humor-induced positive psychology interventions identified the benefits of incorporating daily humor activities to induce laughter reduced depression and increased joy for participants, even months later (Wellenzohn, et al., 2016).

Spend ten minutes each day for five days on the following exercise:

- Write down the three funniest things you have experienced, seen, or heard that day. Provide detail and note how they made you feel.
- If you can't think of anything, search online for funny stories or anecdotes. Social media can be a good source of funny material.
- Write down why you found it funny. The more specific you are, the more effective the exercise will be.
- Write these three funny things at the end of your day. Doing so will foster a new habit and may help you absorb the emotion more as you sleep (Doll, 2021).

- Then share your funny experiences with others (your teams at work or your family/friends). You will not laugh at everything others wrote, but you will most likely gain insights into your teammates that you never had before.

7. Presence

Introduction

Typically, when we speak of presence in the context of Heart Work, we are referencing the state of being conscience in the moments that matter the most. But this passage will go deeper into how we are present amid others.

Gravitas refers to that almost magnetic pull that most inspirational leaders possess. It is an energy that can shift the atmosphere of an entire organization. Though the point may seem obvious and trite to some, gravitas, or the weight of one's presence, can be invaluable in leadership effectiveness. The word is Latin for "weight, substance and importance" (Gray, et al., 2018).

Whether leading a staff meeting or an entire department, it all begins and ends on the strength of a leader's professional presence.   Precious information can fall flat on disengaged, disinterested audiences without presence.   Heart-centered leaders must always establish a clear and positive impression that speaks to who they are as people and leaders, what competencies they bring to the table, and most importantly, what they expect of their team and colleagues.

Have you ever attended a professional gathering, perhaps a networking event, where one person seems to hold court or, some may suggest, *work the room*? This person may not necessarily be the event organizer. Still, you wouldn't necessarily recognize that right away, as they glide comfortably from person to person, conversation to conversation, exuding confidence and self-possession.

Or have you ever attended a staff meeting where a presenter makes a presentation with such high energy that you walk away not only knowing more than you knew but feeling energized and optimistic about your work, goals, and contribution to the company's shared vision?   Have you noticed how the positive energy from one individual can put nearly everyone in a meeting or an event at ease?

And as the atmosphere becomes more relaxed, the most fantastic thing often happens - people talk. They engage. They share ideas and experiences more freely. They relate and open up about their lives, their work, or the things that matter to them most. Meanwhile, this self-assured person, who is usually quite relatable, leans in, discernibly interested to learn all they can from the person or people they are speaking to. They smile. They mirror their captive audience's emotions and rarely even break eye contact. This is presence. And it's a remarkable quality that, though everyone is not born with it, it can be developed and learned.

The Purpose of "Professional" Presence

Social psychologists explain that as humans, we often quickly form lasting opinions about others from very little information. Upon first impressions, we subconsciously ask ourselves, "Can I trust this person?" and "Can I respect this person" (Gray, et al., 2018)? Therefore, leaders must quickly establish their presence as respectable, credible, decisive, and trustworthy (Gray, et al., 2018). As we all know, first impressions rarely come with second chances.

A leader who shows respect and treats others with dignity is non-negotiable when seeking to gain the team's respect. The adage that you get more flies with honey than with vinegar couldn't be more accurate when establishing your professional presence. No one is above exhibiting good manners and respectful communication. These qualities go a long way toward a leader presenting themself as being both congenial and approachable as professional relationships grow. Creative solutions flourish when everyone's effort and perspective are respected.

When leaders demonstrate respect and grace for their team, the environment is primed for those leaders to teach, influence, and share their expertise and learn about their team's competencies. Setting a receptive and respectful dialogue lays the foundation for how a leader can influence and drive their team towards organizational goals.

A professional presence inspires buy-in and added value to your teams (Gray, et al., 2018). Heart-centered leaders know their team must first believe in their leader's ability to lead and to do so effectively. Employees and team members believe in their leadership when they can trust what they say. Simply put, heart-centered leaders who communicate truthfully and follow through on commitments are more effective than those who don't. Employees must believe their leaders will hold up their end of the bargain. Leading a team with empty words and hollow promises is correct. The presence of trustworthy leadership is critical in any organization.

Also, heart-centered leaders who have established a presence of respect and trust can then communicate firm and resolute goals that their team can hang their hat on. Teams are energized when goals are set in a purposeful and achievable way. Sharing a game plan demonstrates competency as a leader (Gray, et al., 2018). A strong, decisive leadership presence is the glue that keeps everyone accountable and focuses everyone's energy toward a common purpose. Heart-centered leadership presence is precious when challenges arise. A team's confidence in their leader's grasp of the issue and ability to exact a plan forward is built on the powerful presence their leader established early on.

The Posture of "Professional" Presence, in a Pandemic

The crisis has a way of revealing those with leadership presence and those who don't. It's fair to say that no problem has upended the entire world and shifted life as we knew it, as the coronavirus pandemic did; at least no crisis in the last 100 years. All at once, the world was forced almost wholly to shut down. Adapting to this chapter in history and business has taken exceptionally creative and resilient levels of leadership. Many surviving industries have sustained themselves by expanding on a previously minimally utilized infrastructure of work-from-home positions. And although this approach seemed to solve the issue of maintaining some connection to employees, it also revealed an entirely new set of challenges. For example, communication tactics that work well among colleagues and team members in a conference room may not translate seamlessly to Brady-Bunch-style quadrants on a computer screen (Schwartzberg, et al., 2020).

How were leaders to virtually connect, lead and influence their team in a meaningful and ongoing way? How would these leaders now redefine their leadership presence through a generally unfamiliar, one-dimensional platform? Would their virtual leadership presence have the same impact? Organizational behavior professor, Andy Molinsky, recommends seeing virtual meetings as "an entirely different context, not simply an in-person meeting or a class on a screen" (Schwartzberg, et al., 2020). Leaders needed to elevate their presence, and many had to become quick studies of video-conferencing etiquette to remain effective.

Pre-covid, one key communication measure of a leader being interested and engaged in the ideas and perspectives of their team was whether that leader adopted a posture that leaned in and maintained eye contact with whoever was speaking. As it turns out, the same is true when establishing a leadership presence virtually. Instead of being tempted to stare into the smiling faces of all attendees, heart-centered leaders should center their gaze on the camera (Schwartzberg, et al., 2020).

This presents as direct eye contact and is vital to reinforce the perception of their interest in what a team member has to say. It also helps increase the impact of a leader's points (Schwartzberg, et al., 2020). When conducting meetings or brainstorming sessions, a leader who maintains eye contact with the little black dot looks directly into every team member's eyes simultaneously.

Leadership presence is also demonstrated by an assertive and robust tone of voice (Schwartzberg, et al., 2020). Again, this was true pre-covid but is even more critical when operating virtually. Often it's best to use a slightly louder than normal tone (without yelling) when video conferencing instead of a conversational volume. By articulating their points clearly, in a firm, authoritative voice, a leader's presence is evinced as confidence, knowledge, and command of the situation at hand.

Leaders who take the time to become more adept at fully utilizing virtual platforms to communicate and present ideas also build confidence among their employees. The chat window, for example, is excellent for linking resource material, answering questions privately or so the whole group can see, or even attaching meeting agendas. This demonstrates preparedness and organization. Virtual meetings present a unique opportunity for a leader to elevate their presence, add context to ideas; and show that a leader is fully present and just as committed as they were in the office environment (Schwartzberg, et al., 2020).

A final note regarding having a leadership presence is a simple reminder – it helps to maintain a sense of humor. Even in these unprecedented times, leaders are still accountable for the morale of their team. And heart-centered leaders know the value of simply letting their team see them smile. This is incredibly impactful when the technology that so many have become nearly reliant on fails us–screens freeze. Signals drop. Attachments don't open. It's okay. Heart-centered leaders keep it all in perspective and remain cool and calm because, often, that's most important anyway. Leaders who understand the importance of their presence understand that their team is taking their cues from them. Current times are challenging and frustrating and have brought on stress levels no one was prepared for. It is during these difficulties that leadership presence matters the most. It's not only okay for leaders to smile in this new virtual business world; it's necessary to maintain a posture that is unflustered and even upbeat as much as possible.

The Power of "Professional" Presence

It's well known that people won't always remember what you say but will never forget how you make them feel (Goman, et al., 2016). When leaders can evoke an emotional response from their team, whether excitement or inspiration, those emotions can be used as an influence to drive results. The built-in power of leadership presence is the ability of leadership to influence and inspire their team toward objectives.

Leadership presence can vary in style, but ultimately it is about the energy and enthusiasm that leaders bring that sets the tone for a team. It's how leaders show up, make others feel, and effectively communicate verbally and non-verbally (Goman, et al., 2016). In many ways, leadership presence is a set of non-verbal communication skills that aren't limited to one personality type. *Soft* skills like posture, eye contact, self-awareness, and active listening help make leaders more effective. Leadership presence inspires team members to be excited about meeting audacious personal and professional goals.

Exercise

Record yourself rehearsing a presentation. Watching your recorded presentation allows you to see yourself as your audience sees you and will enable you to pick up on what's enhancing and detracting from your presence.

Watch your recorded presentation and ask yourself:

- Does my posture convey authority?
- Are non-verbal tics distracting others from paying attention to my message, such as swaying back and forth, tapping my foot, or fidgeting with jewelry?
- Is the tone of my voice firm and confident or tentative and soft? Am I over-using filler words such as "um," or "ah?"
- Is my message being communicated clearly, concisely, and impactful? Does it effectively speak to and connect with my audience?

8. Perseverance

Introduction

In the 2006 film "The Pursuit of Happyness," audiences are given a glimpse into the true story of Chris Gardner. When the story begins, he appears to be your ordinary loving father and husband who desperately struggles to provide the barest necessities for his family. As the story unfolds, it seems he can't catch a break no matter how hard he tries. His car is impounded for unpaid parking tickets. He's robbed (twice), evicted (twice), arrested, used, rejected, and pummeled by life's challenges for most of the 2-hour movie. By all accounts, Chris' life seems like an uphill battle. Nearly every scene is just one failed effort after another, and frankly, it would have been a natural reaction if he had just quit.

Yet, a recurring theme in this seemingly unlucky man's story is his perseverance. This quality manifests in different ways throughout his journey, but it's always in some form. From his stubborn tenacity to solve a Rubik's cube to the consistent effort he put into a failing career selling overpriced medical equipment to doctor's offices and hospitals, to stalking the entrance of a company, meeting an executive, and securing a job interview - Chris remains relentless. Viewers may lose count of how many times he hears the word "No," but what is even more significant is that for every instance of "No," the word just seems to bead off of him like water off a duck. It doesn't seem to penetrate his psyche in any way. He just smiles a genuine smile and keeps going.

Perseverance is the steadfast and continued effort to do or achieve a pursuit, despite difficulties, failure, or opposition. In leadership, everyone should look at perseverance as a core component of one's survival (Seedman). There is no substitute for this quality. Perseverance is an uncompromising commitment to achieving. In leadership, this is a characteristic you must not only possess but also cultivate and reinforce regularly in your team. Challenges, failures, mistakes, and disappointments are a part of life that no one can avoid. But when we adopt a persevering mindset, we can use these setbacks as setups for success by learning and growing from the experience.

Just Ordinary People

I've always loved learning new things about our Earth and the different elements that make up our world, but when I learned about graphite in elementary science class, I was not impressed. It's a soft rock, gray, dull and dusty.   Probably among the most ordinary stones, it can be found along most nature trails, amongst the leaves, dirt, and debris.   It's most commonly used as pencil lead.   Yet, when I realized graphite is identical to the chemical composition of diamonds, it made me give both rocks a second look.   How could something so precious and extraordinary have such a dark and common origin?

Where graphite is soft, diamonds are one of the most complex materials known on Earth.   Where graphite is opaque, dusty, and unremarkable, diamonds are transparent to light, illuminating a magnificent prism of color when light enters it. "How was this possible?" I recall thinking as I held a piece of graphite in my hand, turning it over and examining it for some sign of its potential. I couldn't see it with the naked eye. So what changed it?   What brought out its extraordinary potential?

Pressure. Extreme pressure happens, whether in nature or by artificial means. The pressure was the difference and the reason for this dramatic metamorphosis from graphite to diamond. Hence the expression, *a diamond in the rough*.

The same is true of people. *"Perseverance can turn an ordinary individual into an exceptionally successful expert and leader. On the other hand, the lack of perseverance can turn the most talented individual in the world into one of mediocrity. Simply, perseverance or the lack thereof has a gravitational pull in either a positive or negative direction"* (Seedman). Ordinary, unassuming, average-Joe kind of people of basic means and backgrounds become extraordinary successes every day because they persevered through the pressures of disappointment and failure. The inner potential may not be so evident, but if you pay attention to these individuals' focus and their attitude towards failure and success, it's easy to see what sets them apart.

Walt Disney was fired from the Kansas City Star Newspaper because of a "lack of creativity." He's quoted as saying, "All the adversity I've had in my life, all my troubles and obstacles have strengthened me… You may not realize it when it happens, but a kick in the teeth may be the best thing in the world for you."

When Thomas Edison was interviewed once by a reporter in recognition of his invention of the light bulb, the reporter noted that he'd made 1,000 unsuccessful attempts before his ultimate success. The reporter asked, "How did it feel to fail 1,000 times?" To which Thomas Edison responded, "I didn't fail 1,000 times. The light bulb was an invention with 1,000 steps."

Dr. Martin Luther King, Jr. expressed the concept of perseverance most eloquently when he said, "If you can't fly, then run. If you can't run, then walk. If you can't walk, then crawl. But whatever you do, you have to keep moving forward."

What Disney, Edison, and Dr. King understood is a common revelation that many leaders have. They understood failure's proper relationship to success; failure provides valuable information regarding what does not work (Seedman), which means it's a step closer to what does. These men, in particular, used every failure to inform their choices for their next attempt at reaching their goal. This is the spirit and essence of perseverance. When there's a failure or a setback, it takes deliberate intention, vision, and long-term focus to see that the steps taken towards a goal (the losses) are meaningful and to keep going.

Having a Growth Mindset

Developing perseverance requires dissatisfaction with complacency and holding oneself personally accountable to a plan. The strategies of great leaders often begin with the first step of creating a plan. Once a dream and goal have been defined, it's crucial to organize the project in steps; by separating short-term action plan goals from longer-term achievement goals. Action-plan goals are nested under the higher order of achievement goals (Seedman). By structuring and planning your efforts this way, progress is easily identifiable, and a growth mindset will also begin to develop.

Having a growth mindset is a powerful tool when learning to persevere. When training your mind towards a goal, what you think about matters; being negative, for example, is limiting and can drain focus and creativity. However, thinking positively creates a fertile imagination where solutions and innovations can be born. With a positive perspective, a leader can attack their action plan with consistent effort.

The underlying mechanism is connecting perseverance to high achievement in practice. A growth mindset believes intelligence is malleable and can be developed. Therefore leaders with a growth mindset are always willing to find and dedicate time to focused, deliberate practice towards their goal. Bruce Lee is credited with saying, "I fear not the man who has practiced 10,000 kicks once, but I fear the man who has practiced one kick 10,000 times." This level of practice time is quality time spent on improvement and not cursory time spent superficially, just so that it can be said the time was spent. Having a growth mindset means knowing that *success is not a destination but a journey*. And as stated previously, every step of the journey counts.

Developing Grit in Others

Grit is defined as perseverance and passion for long-term goals, and it can be intentionally cultivated in oneself or others (Merriman, et al., 2017). As a word, it is often used interchangeably with perseverance. However, the concept of grit entails a bit more than a refusal to quit. Grit is courage, resolve, and a steadfast belief in one's vision, even when faced with an opposing reality. Grit is even recognized in the Proverb, "Though a good man falls seven times, he gets back up." This is a quality that can't be impersonated, but it can be learned. Angela Duckworth is a professor of psychology and a pioneer in grit research. She found that *where talent counts once, grit counts twice*. It is the best predictor of success. So as leaders, how can this critical factor be grown in others (Edblad, et al., 2017)?

First, leaders must recognize and make their team aware that success is a long-term commitment. It takes time and consistent, focused practice to achieve anything worthwhile. Second, a leader must learn the team members' passions and interests. It's pretty difficult to "stick it out" with uninteresting tasks. This is why in the interview process, leaders need to dig deeper into the question of hobbies, extracurricular interests, volunteer work, etc. We are so much more than our work experience. Knowing a person's interests tells a leader so much about the person they are considering hiring – information they would otherwise not learn. If a person hasn't yet discovered their areas of interest, it's always good to have them try different things until they find what interests them (Edblad, et al., 2017).

Another means of developing grit and fortitude in others is to challenge them to get comfortable being uncomfortable. It's important to train one's brain for success, so it is essential to set small goals for them. For example, put a small purpose of completing a task in a reasonable amount of time. Then, daily, challenge others to train themselves to achieve the same job more quickly, without sacrificing quality and accuracy. Measure their progress, regular schedule reviews of progress, and celebrate small wins (Edblad, et al., 2017).

Last, a leader should ensure that s/he assembles a team of the same growth mindset, influencing one another to persevere and succeed. Create a culture of "positive peer pressure" where goal-oriented habits are encouraged, belief in the collective vision is the religion, and deliberate practice is the rule, not the exception (Edblad, et al., 2017).

Exercise

Materials Needed: Bag of mini marshmallows and toothpicks. Each participant will have two toothpicks and a mini-marshmallow. The activity aims to demonstrate perseverance, creative problem-solving skills, and seeing a project through to completion. *(This is great for team building)* Participants must use only toothpicks to hold up the marshmallow. This is to be the superior guidance given. Instructors will look for participants who gave up right away or who did it the entire time, along with those who succeeded.

- What annoyed them about the activity?
- If there was a reward, would that change how they participated?
- Did calling it the "Impossible Icebreaker" change how they approached it?
- Why did you spend the whole three minutes trying to lift the marshmallows?
- For those who succeeded, how did they approach the problem?

A way to solve the exercise is to break the toothpicks in half and use all four for equal support or to get with another student to use their toothpicks.

Reference: "The Impossible Icebreaker"
*www.dso.ufl.edudocumentsnsfpIf_Twesigye_Can_So_Can_They_*
A_one_class_lesson_to_help_students_learn_about_perseveran
ce_-_Skylar_Frazier.pdf

9. Mindset

Introduction

Have you ever known something big and extraordinary was about to happen, like closing on your dream home, a wedding, or taking a vacation to a place you've always wanted to go? You were so excited by the impending event that nothing could curb your enthusiasm! You watched the calendar as a child waiting for Christmas. It was all you thought about, talked about, and posted on social media. It didn't matter what else may have been going on; your mind was set on the beautiful thing you'd been waiting on. Your focus was thoroughly trained in anticipation of what was coming, and little else mattered. How powerful are we as human beings to control our focus this way when we have the right motivation?

Mindset is just as remarkable when we aren't waiting anxiously for something specific to happen. Mindset is about where our focus lies generally. Where our focus lies determines our actions or our inactions. A person's mindset accurately reflects who they are, how they want to show up in their lives, and whom they want to become in the future. A mindset can arise out of a person's worldview or personal philosophies. It is our thoughts, focus, awareness, and desires. It shapes our decisions, our attitudes, and our motivations. Simply put, mindset is everything, and it influences everything.

Mindset is also a choice. Having a mindset for growth and progress is not automatic. Most of us, at one time or another, have operated with a mindset that was more reactionary. This mindset can be as emotionally and mentally draining as being stuck on a rollercoaster, having no control and seemingly no ability to get off. However, when we adopt a more proactive mindset, we put ourselves in the driver's seat of our own lives. We choose how to experience the world around us instead of just letting the world drive us.

The sixth-century Chinese philosopher Lao Tzu expressed mindset in the clearest of terms when he said, "Watch your thoughts, they become your words; watch your words, they become your actions; watch your actions, they become your habits; watch your habits, they become your character; watch your character, it becomes your destiny."

Effective Leadership Development

Organizations worldwide spend roughly $356 billion on leadership development efforts. Yet, an analyst firm that surveyed 329 organizations in 2013 found that 75% of the organizations rated their leadership development programs as not very effective. Companies are finding that they are not receiving the return on investment they had hoped for. Further research shows that these programs have been ineffective because they overlook the particular attribute of how leaders think, learn and behave – their mindsets.

For companies to get their money's worth for a quality leadership development program and for it to be effective, the willingness and readiness of their leaders to improve must first be assessed (Gottfredson and Reina, 2020). Simply put, leaders must be willing to learn, adapt and grow whenever an opportunity presents itself. If they are not ready, no amount of development will have any lasting impact. Mindset is the mental lens that dictates what information leaders use to make sense of and navigate the situations they encounter (Gleeson, 2018).

Growth Mindset vs. Fixed Mindset

Having a growth mindset is a belief that people can develop their talents, abilities, and intelligence. However, those with a fixed mindset do not believe that people can change. The latter are often unwilling to fully participate in any lasting adjustments to their leadership style derived from any development program. They feel they know what works, and their minds are fixed. However, having a fixed mindset stagnates growth and is a fruitless mindset for a leader. If a leader can't or won't facilitate change and progress in their team, the individual, the team, and the larger organization will ultimately falter and fail. Like people, companies must continue growing to survive and thrive.

Conversely, having a growth mindset means you are more mentally primed to approach and take on challenges, accept feedback, adopt problem-solving strategies, provide developmental feedback to subordinates, and be effortful and persistent in seeking to accomplish goals (Gottfredson and Reina, 2020). Developing a growth mindset means understanding that even setbacks are opportunities to learn and grow. The core of the growth mindset is about one's attitude towards failure. While some dwell on the disappointment, others rebound and grow in wisdom and intelligence. Researchers in neuroscience refer to it as "brain plasticity," or the ability of the brain to grow new connections and strengthen existing ones just from experience and the actions we take.

There is a direct correlation between mindset and achievement. Leaders with a growth mindset behave differently. They praise their team differently. Instead of rewarding team members with praise for their intelligence, which encourages a fixed mindset, leaders with a growth mindset praise their teams for hard work and effort. This enables the team to take on more and more challenging roles instead of avoiding them. This can also be viewed as having a learning mindset, which directly motivates team members toward increasing their competence and mastering something new.

Deliberative vs. Implemental Mindsets

When developing a mindset toward leadership, it's vital to be open to differing feedback and not be unreceptive to voices and perspectives that disagree with yours. Having a deliberative mindset means being receptive to all kinds of information.

Leaders with this mindset often make better decisions because they are often more balanced and less biased. After all, it was derived from varying points of view (Gottfredson and Reina, 2020). Deliberative leaders know when it's time to heed good counsel.

However, implemental mindsets are more focused on decisions, often prematurely and without sufficient deliberation. This mindset closes itself off to differing ideas and information. As with a fixed mindset, the implemental attitude is counterproductive to cultivating a good team mindset.

Promotion vs. Prevention Mindsets

Leaders with a promotion mindset are focused on winning and gains, and because this is their focus, they are more successful than the negative mindset: prevention. Prevention mindsets avoid problems, whereas the promotion mindset anticipates problems; they focus on their purpose or goal and prioritize making progress toward it. Promotion mindsets don't make time to worry about problems; they are prone to positivity (Gottfredson and Reina, 2020).

Some people in leadership roles are those individuals that are lifelong learners and crave constant opportunities to accept feedback, apply, and grow. Others – maybe not so much. And some are willing but lack self-awareness, so they assume their leadership performance is excellent – and directly linked to the company's good performance. Or, if the performance is lacking, they fail to see their role in that outcome (Gleeson, 2018). A leader's mindset might be one of the most significant predictors of success and one of the most elusive elements to pin down (Clark, et al., 2020).

When leaders develop the mindsets of growth, learning deliberative decision-making and promotion, they can begin to shape their future and team members' futures. Imagination, creativity, and innovative solutions all come from having a mindset that is open and adaptable to change and challenges.

Suppose thoughts determine our actions, and actions drive results, which come full circle to impact our beliefs. In that case, it's essential that, as leaders, we adequately monitor and address our thoughts honestly (Clark, et al., 2020). Self-awareness and taking inventory of our beliefs is the first step. And then, trying on new perspectives can follow. The best leaders see leadership excellence as a constant journey instead of a final destination (Gleeson, 2018).

Exercise

- Reflect on the mindset qualities outlined in this article, considering how you can best integrate them into your mindset.
- Write a short mission sentence on each mindset quality and how it intersects with you. Write your mission sentence on a document along with motivational themes or quotes from people you admire. Put this document somewhere prominent where you can see it and read it daily.
- For the next 28 days, live and breathe your mindset and motivational themes document. Read it in the morning and before bed, talk about it with your confidants, and look for opportunities to practice them in your daily life.

10. Design Thinking

Introduction

When planning a garden, one of the first things you learn is how to know your garden's personality. Shaded areas versus areas that get the most sun. Waterlogged regions where certain root plants would drown, yet perennials thrive. Areas where the soil is nutrient-dense and places where the ground needs to be tilled and fed with compost.

A horticulturalist must know their garden and what herbs or plants are suitable to grow where, whether together with other plants or set apart on their own until they're strong. The concept is similar to how leaders must know their team so well that they design their roles around their natural gifts and abilities. After all, it is the responsibility of leaders to grow and develop their teams to reach their highest potential. What better way to build talent than to maximize the gifts they were born with?

All people have unique gifts and talents that are natural to them. Some people are gifted communicators and would make great teachers. Some have been gifted with extreme patience. Some have an incredible memory, like an elephant. Some have had experiences that have expanded their compassion for the world. These leaders would operate in these capacities for free because it is just who they are.

Design thinking provides an opportunity to capitalize on individual strengths. And as a leader, knowing your team is vital. When applying design thinking as a leader of people, you are leveraging your understanding of those individuals to create a product, strategy, or organic work process, focusing on the end.

Formulating a strategy while creating an environment where people can meet their fullest potential and deliver results can be the most rewarding part of the leadership role. Having the right vision, strategy, resources, and systems in place can mean very little if you don't have the right team for success.

Design thinking provides a human-centered approach to solving problems. It's beneficial in tackling complex problems that are ill-defined or unknown by understanding the human needs involved, re-framing the problem in human-centric ways, creating many ideas in brainstorming sessions, and adopting a hands-on approach in prototyping and testing. These five stages empower leaders and employees and simplify complex dilemmas through collaboration, critical thinking, and effective communication (Dam and Siang, 2021).

For design thinking to be practical, you only need the right mindset, time, and tools. Before you begin applying design thinking to your team, it's precious that you establish your goals. Remember, a meaningful solution has a purpose, is functional, is understandable, and fits the context (White, 2020).

In defining your goals, ask yourself and your collaborator questions about the overarching theme on which collaborative thinking will be centered; questions like (White, 2020):

- How might we identify a new strategic direction for our company that suits the current global situation?
- How are global problems affecting our business?
- What are these problems?
- Which business goals should we consider?
- Can we define our most important goal?

- Why is the current way no longer appropriate?

- What would happen if we did nothing?

- What currently works and is worth keeping?

- Has anything not worked in the past that should be avoided?

These are not questions that can quickly be answered when starting. Leaders will revisit these questions throughout the development, and everyone will evolve, change perspectives, and take on differing opinions as they go through the process.

Also, leaders and facilitators must remain inclusive and encourage collaboration throughout the process.   Listen and guide your team rather than instruct. Let the overarching purpose fuel your positivity under challenging moments.   Look for opportunities to link ideas through increased understanding. Take notes and record "think tank" sessions.

Empathize

The first phase of implementing design thinking is to develop an empathetic understanding of the problem. Researching so you can observe, engage and empathize with people can be extremely helpful in understanding their experiences and motivations. Set aside your assumptions and be open to new insight about the needs of others. Team members who are naturally good observers of people and their needs may be well suited for this role.

Define

This is an opportunity to analyze your observations from the previous phase. At this stage, leaders and collaborators are seeking to clearly define the problems that have been identified and name the problem as a statement in a human-centered way. Team members with strong analytical skills who enjoy solving puzzles or riddles are great at evaluating and organizing information.

Ideate

This is when solutions are flushed out and made more tangible and less abstract. This should be a deliberately inclusive effort. The practice of visualization techniques like mind mapping is functional when brainstorming. Groupthink can suppress creative thought, so allow collaborators to write their ideas down for 20-30 minutes, giving them uninterrupted time to process and formulate their ideas for solutions. Then, bring the team back together for a vote on ideas, discussing and debating the most popular solutions, but not ruling out anything until the next phase. Leaders should ensure that this is a collaborative effort by providing everyone contributes a vote and a perspective.

Prototyping

This phase is about ruling out ideas that may not correctly or fully address the problem earlier defined.   This doesn't mean the opinions are dead on arrival.   It just means the idea should be tabled for later discussion, or details need to be fleshed out more.

Again, this is a collaborative effort.   Leaders should set an expectation of respectful and productive debate about all ideas. When ideas are ruled out, it should be expressed that it's a personal rejection and that there may just be better solutions.

Testing

Finally, a solution has been narrowed down, and it's time to see how adequately it solves that problem. Ask for feedback from the people observed during the Empathy phase.   Or use other individuals who represent the target market. Listen for feedback on how the solution can be improved before implementation (Dam and Siang, 2021).

Design Thinking takes time and persistence, but it's worth the effort. It is not necessarily a linear process where each step fits quaintly and seamlessly transitions to the next phase (White, 2020). The process is usually more hopscotch than a linear path, where different stages are revisited, problems may need more clarity, and ideas may need to be reimagined. It is the job of leadership to remind team members that the end goal of a solid solution for the people being served is worth the effort.

Exercise

What problem have you observed in your career or community that you believe you could solve? Formulate your situation as a human-centered statement and share it with two or three colleagues. Apply design thinking; record your process, and observe how that approach differs from past methods.

11. Greatness

Introduction

"Great leadership is transforming. Leaders who inspire others to be great perpetuate an exchange of greatness that makes it fun to go to work every day."

Great leaders challenge their employees with tasks outside their regular jobs; it may take them longer to complete, but a true leader is patient and encouraging. As employees become more comfortable, leaders know their efficiency will improve. In time, a leader may delegate similar tasks to their employee, increasing their responsibilities and preparing them for future opportunities. Allowing employees this room to grow is an exciting way to develop them, even if things move slowly at the beginning.

Leaders who look for opportunities to grow their employees' skill set and experience are inspirational. Employees' confidence in their abilities increases, as does their willingness to take on other challenges. Great leaders are exceptional and make exceptional coaches as well. A good coach inspires one to think differently in sports or business by asking more reflective questions. Coaches educate on a problem generally, perhaps regarding the behind-the-scenes information of how a situation came to be. But then these leaders ask the employee, based on this new information, how they would handle complex issues.

Exceptional leaders are also the best cheerleaders. Not all, but many people need a pat on the back from time to time. An outstanding leader will happily provide that boost of support and encourage others to do the same.

Giving Good Encouragement

Encouraging people outside their comfort zone and watching them meet the challenge should be celebrated. Many employees need that gentle push and usually appreciate it in the long run. It is a great honor for exceptional leaders to provide that inspiration out of their comfort zone and into a sense of accomplishment. Most leaders credit the push of a previous leader, teacher, or coach in their life development for why they have enjoyed many successes. These leaders are just paying forward the good fortune of a good push. *"If your actions inspire others to dream more, learn more, do more, and become more, you are a leader."* - John Q. Adams

From the employee's perspective, it's an incredible feeling when the individual entrusted with your development, your leader, challenges you, and you feel the fireworks of "aha" moments going off inside as you learn to see something different.

Greatness in leaders is expressed through a passion for being extraordinary. They think confidently and positively about everything they do. We all know that positive thinking can set off a chain reaction of positive thoughts, events, and outcomes to come our way. How we respond to our team members when the stakes are high, and the consequences matter inspires courage.

Greatness is never a one-person job. Greatness is the ability to elevate effective, consistent, and empathic communication in all we endeavor. The essence of all that we do should be thoughtful, deliberate, and intentional. There should be an organized rhythm and clarity about the purpose so that all team members feel included and engaged in every aspect of the organization.

Communicating Greatness

There is no path to profitability without constructive communication. Great leaders are generally effective communicators. Profitability comes from productivity, efficiency, management, discipline, and managing our time and business. If we make a meaningful contribution to this world, we must value our time, the time of others, and the energy it takes to get to where we want to go. A true leader's mindset says we cannot afford to allow poor communication and resentments to get in the way of our efficiency and profitability.

The mindset necessary for achieving greatness is understanding that success is *not* your ultimate goal. This goal is too small and unilateral. To strive for excellence, you must be well-rounded and humble. You must be more interested in building a *cause* that touches people, not just the bottom line. Be willing to step out of the box. Strive to be a pioneer, a trendsetter, a game-changer, and a radical thinker who is deeply driven to make this world a better place.

Exercise

Answer these questions: What is the enterprising thing you will do for free if income is not necessary? Who is the top leader or innovator who has achieved *Greatness* in that industry, which you also respect? How can you use that person's rise to greatness to inform your journey and inspire your success?

"You were put on this earth to achieve your greatest self, to live out your purpose, and to do it courageously." - *Steve Maraboli*

12. Psychological Wellness

Introduction

The world is filled with amazingly talented and gifted people from all walks of life who have lived incredibly entire lives; filled with love, joy, support, and grace. They are charismatic, lively, and outgoing, and it's as if they've never met a stranger. The world is also filled with talented and gifted people who are emotionally broken, anxious about the future or burdened by past mistakes. Their lives are filled with episodes of trauma, disappointment, and loneliness. They feel alone even in crowded rooms because they think no one can ever really understand them.

What's interesting about these two types of people I've described is that they're not necessarily two separate groups. They can be the same person. A deeply supported and loved person can still suffer from trauma's lasting impacts. A severely lonely and depressed person can also be outgoing. And let's be clear, psychological wellness and mental health are not the same things, but we want to be healthy in both dimensions to live an active and fulfilling life.

Considering the many nuances of the human brain's ability to cope and survive, it should never be assumed – just by looking at the surface – what a person's lived experiences are from day to day. Based on what can be observed, assumptions about a person's psychological wellness can be why an individual's invisible struggles go unchecked and unaddressed.

Add to this old normal a new normal, the long-term stress we've endured to varying degrees globally due to the Coronavirus pandemic. Our very brains have had to be rewired as we watched the world stop, totally paralyzed by this pandemic. Previous statistics from 2016 reported that about 20% of Americans reportedly had a mental illness; that number has skyrocketed to nearly 50% of Americans who say Covid-19 has been triggering and damaging their mental health. Whereas psychological wellness may not have been a significant concern in the workplace a few short years ago, ignoring the mental health of the people that make up an organization (from management to entry-level) is no longer an option (Lipkin,

2020).   Organizations and leaders must show genuine interest and make the necessary effort to proactively support their teams' and themselves' psychological wellness and mental health.

What is Psychological Wellness?

The author of a study published in Applied Psychology: Health and Well-Being describes psychological well-being as "the combination of feeling good and functioning effectively." High psychological well-being refers to a person feeling happy and doing well. These individuals live with a sense of satisfaction in their lives. They are ideal for a team setting because they work with a sense of pride and purpose (Morin, 2020).

Unfortunately, nearly half of us have not been "doing well" for many months or even years, including leaders and managers. For leaders to effectively address the needs of their employees, they must first take a serious inventory of their psychological state. It is of the utmost importance that leaders remember that they are human and that while balancing the needs of the business with those of its employees is vitally important, a leader must also find the space to prioritize their health as well; find their support, and not go at it alone (Lipkin, 2020)

The Cost of Ignoring Psychological Wellness

Unhealed, unaddressed psychological issues can be like walking around on broken bones which haven't adequately healed or have healed in a misaligned position. It is painful. Without proper attention, that pain and stress can seep into and affect our attitudes, our ability to focus and engage with our work (which means our performance suffers), and our ability to communicate effectively and cope with challenges. Absenteeism and presenteeism increase, while productivity decreases, overall morale plummets, and so does the company's the profit/impact.

Psychological wellness is essential for both people and profit since it directly impacts the health of a company's bottom line. More than 300 million people suffer from depression globally. Depression and anxiety cost the global economy an estimated $1 trillion yearly in lost productivity. You read that right; that's Trillion, with a capital "T."

The good news is, however, according to the World Health Organization, it is estimated that for every $1 invested into creating and supporting mental health disorders, there is a return of $4 in improved health and productivity. Research shows that nearly 86 percent of employees treated for depression report improved work performance. And in some studies, treatment of depression has been shown to reduce absenteeism and presenteeism by 40 to 60 percent. A healthier workforce also means more retention and less turnover, which is another cost-saving benefit. Healthier employees don't get sick as often and have fewer on-the-job accidents. These are all cost-saving benefits. Therefore, investing in support, training, and treatment for mental health is a virtual no-brainer (Sime, 2019).

The Benefits of Workplace Wellness Programs

Workplace wellness programs can uniquely identify those at risk, connect them to treatment, and put in place support to help people reduce and manage stress. The workplace is an optimal setting to create a culture of wellness since communication structures are already in place and social support networks are available. Employers can offer incentives to reinforce healthy behaviors, and they can measure and track progress. Workplace health promotion programs have been successful, especially mental and physical health interventions (Mental Health in the Workplace, 2019). By addressing mental health issues in the workplace, employers can, directly and indirectly, reduce health care costs for their business, shareholders, and employees.

How Leaders Can Best Support Psychological Wellness

Though most business leaders are not also trained psychologists, being a leader may call for some therapeutic asking and listening. With the proper company-sponsored training, leaders can learn to recognize the signs and symptoms of stress and depression in team members and encourage them to seek help from qualified mental health professionals. It's not expected that you would have all the answers, but the goal is to listen and be empathetic.   Then, point employees in the right direction of resources offered by the company.   Leaders may even want to share their struggles to relate when appropriate.   We must normalize the conversation about psychological wellness and mental health for everyone's well-being.

How Companies Can Support Psychological Wellness

Fortunately, many employers are enhancing emotional and mental health benefits to meet the needs of their employees. Aside from offering health insurance with no or low out-of-pocket costs for depression medications and mental health counseling, employers are learning to be more proactive about on-the-job support.   Such measures include offering subsidized clinical screenings for depression, hosting seminars or workshops that address stress management techniques (like mindfulness, breathing exercises, and meditation), creating and maintaining dedicated, quiet spaces for relaxation activities when employees need a reset, and even giving employees opportunities to participate in decisions about issues that affect job stress.

As leaders, when addressing psychological wellness, the most important thing is to remind your team that we are all human and, though no one has all the answers, help is available. We're in this together, and much can be accomplished when we all work together.

Exercise

Caring for others through volunteering has been shown to reduce stress and depression and increase psychological wellness by promoting a sense of purpose. It also occupies the mind and body, which is an added benefit. The suggested exercise for this lesson is volunteering at a local charity and documenting your experience from a mental health perspective. How did you feel when you arrived? What did you do? How were you helpful? How did you feel when you left? Will you return? Get your team involved; there is an inner light that shines when we serve others and even brighter when we do it together.

13. Emotional Wellness

Introduction

Emotional wellness relates to an awareness, understanding, and acceptance of your emotions and your ability to manage effectively through challenges and change. It is critical to our overall health and well-being and, therefore, crucial to the health of any organization.

A key component to emotional wellness is letting go of past disappointments or mistakes and tempering anxieties about an uncertain future. Instead, emotional health emphasizes being present in the now. This is commonly referred to as mindfulness and is very important for emotional well-being. As leaders, we must encourage our employees to maintain their perspective and not overwhelm themselves with what is out of their control. Employees who adopt this balanced and practical point of view are less stressed and can more readily focus on their personal and professional objectives.

The rapid pace of business, and the world at large, is overwhelming. It's natural to feel overwhelmed, and it's ok to slow down and assess where you are emotional as you navigate it all. Being emotionally well doesn't necessarily mean you're happy all the time, but rather that you're self-aware and able to shift to feel and be better (Raab, 2019). It is difficult, if not impossible, to meet the demands of our lives now, let alone attain our fullest potential, when we are weighed down with emotional baggage.

Perspective of a Growing Leader

In her careful wisdom, my grandmother once said, "It's not what they call you; it's what you answer to." This has been a philosophy I've held near and dear ever since, and it's a belief I carried with me into adulthood and my career in leadership. Of course, at the time, my beloved grandmother was counseling me on how to cope with the neighborhood bully. However, the advice still rings true in many other challenges I've faced, professionally and personally – that had more to do with "the bully within" than any bully without. There have been times when my leadership insecurities have gotten the best of me, and I've had to quiet that nagging inner bully who would remind me of past mistakes. It would tell me that my future opportunities would be limited because of these mistakes, and whatever opportunities I did get, I would probably just mess those up too.

This inner nagging was relentless. It made it difficult to focus on work or on supporting my teams. But then I remembered my grandmother's words; I realized I'd been answering to terms that didn't reflect me. I'd been letting my insecurities tear me down. But the truth was, my mistakes had been the most significant lessons of my career. They had shaped me into the patient, empathetic and knowledgeable leader I'd become. I'd also been "answering to" the notion that my weaknesses were problematic. I had solved more problems than I'd created in my career and life. Many relied upon and trusted me in the areas in which I was most decisive. This inner bully had to go!

I decided to take charge of my internal narrative. I decided to take a proactive approach to care for my emotional wellness and practice mindfulness, that is, being present and letting go of the past regrets or worries about the future. I learned that taking walks outside and breathing deeply was like medicine when I felt stress or anxiety. I also decided to express gratitude for those experiences that shaped me. This perspective gave me the resilience I needed to bounce back. Being human means having challenges and problems, and life is about how we cope and recover from those challenges that determine our emotional wellness.

Humanness

With constant technological innovations and the immediacy of the business environment nowadays, it can be easy to forget that, though everything else is moving at a breakneck speed 24/7, we cannot and should not expect to do the same. We are not our laptops. We are not soulless, lifeless robots; we cannot drive on empty tanks. We need moments to step back and take inventory of ourselves to perform optimally and deliver results. Even high-performing, top-notch Type A personalities need a break from time to tlme, and it may not be a scheduled break. Our employees need to know we know it's okay not to be okay. It's only human.

Emotional wellness is indeed a workplace issue; ignoring that reality can cause problems to fester and create a damaging ripple effect. It is the responsibility of leaders to be mindful of the pressures our workforce may be experiencing at any given moment. Recognize if there has been a shift in attitude or behavior – regular check-ins just to ask, "How are you?" And listening to their response is essential. Make an effort to understand what your employees' individual needs may be and what they value, and empathize sincerely at all times. As leaders entrusted with the growth and development of other people, we must allow for the necessary adjustments and provide the time and space our employees need to achieve emotional wellness (Lipkin, 2020). Challenges help us relate and connect with our employees in ways that can't be overstated. As leaders, it's not only ok to use our humanness to link to our employees in moments of difficulty; it's fundamentally necessary.

Personal reflection: *For example, I've learned from experience that sometimes I just need to talk it out when I have been overwhelmed and need to cope. I want to be listened to while I unload and unpack it all. Often, I might need some fresh air. So I may take a walk. These have been my coping mechanisms. So, when my employees have expressed similar distress, the first thing I give them is my ear. I listen to whatever they have bubbling up to the surface and hear for ways I can best support them. I lean in. I ask permission to hug if they need it. I nod to indicate understanding and maintain eye contact, so they know I am interested in their well-being. No subject is off-limits, as I assure them of the strictest confidence. Once they've gotten it out, I advise they take a 10-15 minute walk or drive and step away. Again, I recommend this because that is what I have needed in my moments of difficulty. If they needed something more from me, I did my best to oblige them. In those moments, my priority is to support them in any way I can and help them regain space of emotional balance.*

The Worth of Wellness

While prioritizing the needs of employees is of the utmost importance, it is also the duty of leadership to balance those needs with the organization's needs. As leaders, we can never take our eye off the ball regarding business objectives and the benefits of managing an emotionally and mentally healthy workforce, which directly correlates to a healthy bottom line.

Employees experiencing chronic stress are more susceptible to illness, injury, and burnout. They are also more prone to error, irritable, and less productive. For these reasons and others, these employees represent a cost burden that, when multiplied by many, can eat away at a company's bottom line. However, emotionally well employees who exhibit increased decision-making and communication skills are more productive, make fewer mistakes, and are more likely to be physically healthy. These emotionally balanced individuals, therefore, represent cost savings to the company.

Supporting employees to care for their emotional wellness positively influences company culture and directly impacts the company's quality of service (Curtis, 2017).

Exercise

Journal Question: How have you handled the COVID-19 pandemic? From being in quarantine to the daily fear and uncertainty of the virus to the grief over lost loved ones and suffering over the loss of life as we knew it, it's been a lot to handle. How have you coped? What has this experience taught you, if anything, about what matters to you? What has this experience taught you about YOU?

14. Social Wellness

Introduction

Happiness is an often overlooked aspect of health, but happiness is a critical component of our mental and emotional wellness, which supports our physical fitness. Happiness reduces stress, depression, high blood pressure, and obesity. Employees who are healthy and happy have fewer absences and better production.

Quality relationships play a significant role in our happiness and lend to a person's life quality. Social wellness is about building and maintaining positive relationships that add value to our lives. Leaders can address social health in the workplace by encouraging people to engage with their colleagues in collaborative efforts and help one another when necessary (Amador de San Jose, 2019).

Social psychologists have studied the human need for social connection for many years. It's been found that feeling a social bond is an essential intrinsic motivator of human existence. Abraham Maslow's hierarchy of needs includes a sense of belonging as a significant need that motivates human behavior, like food, shelter, and safety (Kohll, 2018).

From children on the playground, working adults in corporate settings, and older adults living in the same retirement community, seeking social connection is a lifelong journey. Our social links profoundly influence our mental health, workplace engagement, and productivity. It affects us most when defining who we are and whom we want to be in and out of our careers.

Since full-time employees spend most of their time at work, workplace relationships are significant to employee well-being. It's about more than just "getting along" with a colleague. It's about connection. Humans crave contact and fellowship with other people (Bevacqua, 2019).

The Disconnect of Technology

Unfortunately, the workplace can be very lonely for many employees. Since business relies on near-immediate communication, most employees utilize email and instant messaging more than their interpersonal skills. Although the technology was meant to connect people worldwide, it can also create a disconnect with people working in the adjacent cubicle.

Now, with so much of the workforce working remotely, it is more vital than ever for leaders to understand how critical social relationships among colleagues are and not let anyone feel isolated. Leaders can create a balanced work environment where collaboration and communication are still encouraged, even when co-workers are in different locations (Kohll, 2018).

Employees want to feel connected and included, and being socially isolated can lower productivity. Leaders must proactively seek ways to have team members working remotely to continue to feel that they are a part of a whole and a part of a team that values their contribution.

Social Benefits

Supporting employee social well-being is essentially a matter of offering your workers good social benefits. Implemented correctly, these benefits can be easy to deliver and relatively cost-effective.

What constitutes a "social benefit?" There is a wide range of options, and your program can be tailored to your employees' specific needs and preferences. Some examples include: holding monthly lunches, hosting after-work socials, throwing companywide success celebrations, or granting employees charity days during which they can donate their time to a good cause together (Jackson, 2020). Also, consistently treating your team with respect, appreciation, and compassion works just as much.

It's so important that team members build trust and share in the vision for the team and the organization. Social wellness is achieved when people connect and nurture those connections.   People are generally much happier and healthier when they click, which directly translates to quality work performance (Kohll, 2018).

How Leaders Can Support Social Wellness

Unfortunately, forming relationships in the workplace can seem a bit awkward or forced for many employees. No one wants to overstep boundaries, and sometimes finding ways to bond with colleagues on a personal level can be challenging. This is why leaders must promote a workplace culture that encourages social interaction and helps employees connect. Leaders can do this by emphasizing the importance of social and emotional well-being in their workplace wellness program (Bevacqua, 2019).

A workplace wellness program can take on many forms. Leaders can encourage team-building exercises to strengthen team camaraderie and rapport, whether a board game or a game of sports trivia. Leaders may implement a wellness challenge where employees are challenged to walk together for a certain amount of time or distance to bring awareness to a worthy social cause. Or implement something as simple as designating a quiet space in the workplace to decompress and socialize.

The purpose of supporting social wellness is to simply create a safe, judgment-free space where employees can freely communicate their needs, feelings, or thoughts. It also offers the opportunity for employees to listen to one another. Leaders should even share transparent moments about their challenges. Employees generally work best in an environment where they can feel supported and enjoy positive interactions with others while participating as an interdependent piece of the giant puzzle of humankind (Optimum Performance Institute, 2013).

Exercise

Journal about a time when you have been the "new kid on the block," entering a new team for the first time. What ice breaker solidified that you are now a team member? Was it relating to a co-worker about a shared interest? Or was it listening to a colleague share a challenge you linked to? How did this experience strengthen your commitment to the team?

15. Physical Wellness

Introduction

Almost everyone is familiar with the emergency instructions flight attendants provide over the plane's intercom before taking off. "In the unlikely event of a sudden loss of cabin pressure, oxygen masks will drop from the panel above your head…Please secure your mask by covering your nose and mouth before helping others, such as children or elderly passengers."

The premise is straightforward - to assist others effectively, you must first prioritize your wellness. The same is true in leadership. For leaders to be truly effective and successful in their leadership roles and to lead their teams toward personal and professional goals, they must first establish, prioritize and pursue their health and wellness goals.

There's a similar old saying: "You can't pour from an empty vessel." Again, heart-centered leaders know that they must fill their vessel before they can pour into others. And the absolute best way to achieve a full vessel is through physical fitness and practicing good eating habits.

Though the United States is among the most wealthy developed countries on the planet, the health of its citizens does not reflect this advantage. The undue burden of sickness and disease on business is evident. From excessive sick leave for chronic illness - which reduces productivity to the skyrocketing cost of healthcare premiums paid by employers to product recalls and environmental hazards that harm communities and citizens - we persistently check all the wrong boxes as one of the most unhealthy modern societies on the planet. But we don't have to be.

With so many modern conveniences, we can be a healthier world. Leaders within organizations have both a personal and a professional responsibility to do their part and lead their workforce by setting an example of wellness.

Individuals in leadership positions owe it to themselves to take care of themselves.

Being "Fit" to Lead

Leadership begins within, with self-governance or self-leadership. Discipline. Consistency. Resilience. There's no better way to *exercise* these qualities than through physical wellness – pun intended. Leaders who exercise and have healthy habits generally handle stressful situations better. Eating well and exercising regularly boost one's ability to control the inherent stressors that come with the responsibility of leading others.

Staying healthy reduces stress and anxiety, improves sleep, and boosts the body's immune system so leaders can readily respond to their employees' and day-to-day business needs. In addition to the apparent benefits of physical wellness, statistics show executives who are physically fit are also considered to be more heart-centered leaders than those who aren't. Again, because of the reduced stress and increased ability to handle the demands of their position, these leaders are viewed as more effective in their roles by their peers and their employees.

Even more beneficial to leaders, a healthful lifestyle enhances brain function, in which case leaders are shown to be more decisive and thoughtful. Their reasoning, problem-solving ability, and creativity are enhanced, and their memory is improved. This is the result of exercise on the rejuvenation of the brain. The brain creates new blood vessels through the cerebral cortex, which oxygenates the brain and enhances brain function.

Leaders who exercise also benefit from endorphins, so-called happy hormones that flood the brain with feelings of goodwill. This makes for more comfortable, kinder, empathetic, thoughtful leaders and communicators. Emotionally and mentally, people who prioritize their health live more balanced lives. These leaders have sustained energy output and are generally more physically resilient during cold and flu seasons.

It should be noted that making physical health and wellness a priority doesn't need to be time-consuming. Sharon McDowell-Larsen, an exercise physiologist with the Center for Creative Leadership, emphasizes that daily mini-workouts for 5-10 minutes can be easily integrated into the busy schedule of most leaders and is more effective than hour-long exercises once or twice a week. Ms. McDowell-Larsen further details five key ways to make regular exercise a habit:

- **Do less, more often.** Short stints of moderate daily exercise are better for maintaining energy and boosting performance than an hour performed only on the weekends.

- **Break up the day.** Find little ways to increase your activity throughout the day: Walk while talking on the mobile phone, take frequent stretch breaks, park at the far end of the lot, and take the stairs.

- **Keep track.** Log your workouts: what you did and for how long. You'll be able to track progress, set goals, and stay motivated.

- **Be flexible.** Take advantage of an open slot in your calendar whenever it appears. If someone else keeps your calendar, ask them to schedule workouts for you.

- **Mix it up.** While your stationary bike or treadmill may be convenient, you will likely get bored. When the weather is nice, go outdoors. Play a sport or a game of tag. Try a new exercise class or go dancing (A Leader's Best, 2020).

Wellness At Work

Leaders and the companies they manage have a vested interest in the health and wellness of their employees also. The latest reporting indicates that employers spend upwards of $8 billion annually on wellness programs. Add that investment to the workplace provides the most optimal opportunity for employee wellness efforts. One would think America's epidemic of obesity, chronic illness, and skyrocketing health care costs would eventually begin to trend in the opposite direction at some point. However, a clear gap exists between companies' time and resources and the negligible number of employees who take advantage of these programs and prioritize their health. Heart-centered leadership can impact this disconnect - leading by example and creating initiatives that drive employee participation.

Great leaders can inspire change and growth and challenge their teams toward goals great and small. When leaders have a wellness reputation, it inevitably piques the interests of some team members to create new habits and establish better health choices for themselves. And when leaders provide incentives for wellness, such as competitions for steps taken in a day, it creates a ripple effect that can impact the whole team. Leaders do these sorts of things because the well-being of their employees matters to them, and when employees know that they matter to their leadership, it creates a bond and sets a new tone for the overall business culture (Kurland, 2020).

A New Day

Decades ago, companies largely ignored their workforce's physical, mental and spiritual health in favor of more "economic" concerns. However, our experience today is quite different. Most heart-centered leaders and companies recognize the need to emphasize a holistic approach to caring for team members. They understand this includes more than annual performance reviews on goals and accomplishments. Leadership teams must see the whole employee, not just once a year but every day.

When this leadership level is exhibited well, retention and engagement numbers will soar. Even more importantly, leaders will know that they have contributed to their team's overall well-being and helped to create self-care habits that will last a lifetime (Purcell, 2016).

Exercise

Psychologists say it takes 28 days to create or break a habit. Commit to incorporating two of the five critical practices toward better physical health as listed by Ms. McDowell-Larsen for 28 days. Then add the third habit the next week and a fourth the following week until you have incorporated all five. Keep a journal to notate your activity and how you feel - mind, body, and spirit. Are you sleeping better? Do you have the same cravings? Last, invite a colleague or several to join you on your journey.

16. Listen

Introduction

Recently, I decided to try my hand at something new that seemed all the rage while we were in quarantine in 2020. I decided to bake banana bread! I don't bake often, but I have baked before, and I thought this seemed a simple enough recipe to try. But I wanted to make my banana bread with a twist; I wanted blueberry banana bread. I checked my fridge to ensure I had butter, salt, flour, baking soda, eggs…the regular baking staples, and ripe bananas. I didn't have sugar, vanilla, and my twist, frozen blueberries. So the evening before I planned to bake, I swung by our local grocer to get the items I needed. I could find the sugar and blueberries quite quickly, but I couldn't find the vanilla anywhere. Perhaps all the banana bread baking I'd heard about was causing a vanilla shortage.

So, I found the nearest attendant and said, "Excuse me, could you point me in the direction of…". As I spoke, she glanced at my shopping basket with the blueberries and sugar. She cut me off, "Aisle 4." I was confused. "I'm sorry?" She answered without looking at me this time, "Aisle 4. Pancakes, right?" I was more confused.

"No, ma'am, I was going to ask where I could find the…." She cut me off again, "Syrups on aisle four too, just above the pancake mix." I respond again, "Ma'am, I am not making pancakes…."

"Or is it aisle 6?" she questioned herself, cutting me off a third time. She then proceeded to walk away as if showing me to aisle 6… or possibly 4. I followed her.

"There have been people here all day getting ready for the Pancake Breakfast tomorrow morning at the community center so that we might be out of both…" she seemed more interested in speaking to herself than me. "Vanilla!" I blurted out from behind her. She turned around; now, she looked confused.

"Oh, well, that's on aisle 12," she gestured. "Thank you. I just came from aisle 12." I turned, pretty frustrated, leaving my basket to be re-shelved and leaving the store. I never got around to making the blueberry banana bread.

The ability to communicate effectively is a skill often taken for granted. However, it remains an irreplaceable aspect of building productive working relationships among employees, management, staff, vendors, and customers. Listening, literally with our ears or metaphorically with understanding, is at the heart of every relationship and every human interaction and is the only way to communicate thoughtfully. Though well-intentioned and willing to help, this grocery store clerk ignored this basic tenet of customer service in our brief interaction. She overlooked the core courtesy of simply listening.

Don't Mistake Hearing for Listening

In today's hurried climate, there is so much information overload and digital distraction that it can be tempting to ignore a person's questions or concerns. Especially if we believe we can anticipate what that person, be it a colleague, an employee, or a customer, might be suggesting before they've finished speaking. We may tune out or glaze over even while they are talking, perhaps catching every other word but only really listening for what we feel is the gist of what is being said. And once we think we've got it, we free our minds to wander to other things that might feel more pressing. We are just waiting for the speaker to take a breath so we can interject our already formulated, canned response and move on with our day. Or worse, interrupt the speaker to speed things along. We aren't listening to gain information so that we can provide thoughtful feedback. We are only listening to respond. It's certainly not a respectful, effective, or kind communication style.

The irony is that this impatience towards accurate communication delays progress since parties have to repeat themselves, or the ineffective communication leads to mistakes that need to be undone. In leadership, we must remember that respect and patience are mutually beneficial. One of the easiest ways to frequently exhibit concern is to (really) listen to our teams and colleagues.

"We think we listen, but rarely do we listen with real understanding or true empathy. Yet listening, of this very kind, is one of the most potent forces for change that I know," says Carl Rogers, an American psychologist and one of the founders of the humanistic approach to psychology.

The Art of Listening

The act of listening requires intention and engagement with the person you are speaking with and listening to. First, it is always best practice to make and maintain eye contact with the person speaking. This indicates they have your undivided attention and that you are interested in the information being shared. Make sure you reflect on what is shared. When you mirror or remember what the speaker has shared, you paraphrase in a way that allows the speaker to clarify their point.

Look for opportunities to relate to the information, if possible, without redirecting the focus to you; keep the focus on the speaker's point. For example, be empathic if they share their experience about a difficulty. Or, if they share an idea, give their idea consideration and share your thoughts based on the merits. Ask good, open-ended questions and then listen to the response. Don't be afraid to lean in, so the speaker knows their answer to your question genuinely matters to you. Be the kind of leader and set the example that shows you understand that everyone's perspective has value (Toledo et al., 2018). School children who are just beginning to learn how to communicate their thoughts and feelings share the most astute and practical perspectives –

until proven otherwise, it should be assumed that everyone has something constructive and valuable to add.

The Value of Listening

Listening is the cornerstone of productivity as it boosts confidence and reduces errors. It is also vital to build one's professional network (Toledo et al., 2018).

Listening means gathering the facts and seeking to understand emotions, and non-verbal communication, such as body language and facial expressions associated with your topic. Paying full attention requires follow-up questions to ensure you fully understand the whole picture. To listen is to be attentive (Chaffold, 2020).

When leaders exercise listening skills, it enables them to acquire facts to make sound decisions that affect the team or the entire organization. Leaders who are attentive to employees can discover what aspects of a task they find most rewarding or challenging. This is valuable information as it informs the leader about how they can motivate their team, build morale and improve productivity. Listening also reduces conflict. When employees feel that they're being listened to, they feel respected and are more willing to share their feelings and opinions, leaving less room for misunderstandings (Tingum, 2019).

Frankly, the benefits of being a good listener as a leader or in everyday life are endless. Though researchers estimate that most people only remember 25-50% of what we hear, this is evidence that highly successful people hone this vital life skill.

Exercise

Paraphrasing and Confirmation Team Building Exercise:
Paraphrasing involves repeating what the speaker said to you to gain confirmation. Five members stand in a group in the "storyline" exercise. The leader asks for the title of the story from the audience. The game begins when the first person gives the first few lines of the story. The person sitting next to her must continue the story when the leader points to her. If s/he does not repeat the lines precisely as her teammate has spoken, the leader calls her "out," and she must sit down.

The story is complete when all five members have had an opportunity to repeat their team members' story additions and add their own. The leader can call a member out if what s/he is adding does not make sense or if he incorrectly tells his teammates part of the story.

Reference: https://smallbusiness.chron.com/activelistening-exercises-team-building-18679.html

17. Engage

Introduction

Employee engagement is a valuable and necessary skill set of leadership. And it's a 2-way street.   It allows leaders to get to know and assess their employees, and it also allows employees to understand and evaluate their leadership, the company, and the expectations set for them.   Engagement doesn't require a formal process.   It can be as easy as asking employees how they feel about their role and position or goals for the following year. Just asking these basic questions and being genuinely engaged and interested in the feedback makes leaders more trusted and helps team members feel valued.

An article in the New York Daily News reported that nearly 70% of U.S. employees are miserable at work.   According to the story, research conducted by the Gallup Poll suggests that most Americans dislike or feel disengaged on the job (Taylor, et al., 2015). The study showed that a consistent complaint was a lack of leadership engagement. Employees simply felt they were "just numbers" who clocked in, clocked out, and passed the time looking for other opportunities. To classify this as miserable is an understatement.   How could an employee ever reach their highest potential in that environment? How can companies ever benefit from all that untapped potential if they rarely even take the time to engage their employees?

Make Engagement a Priority

Engaging employees should be an ongoing, regular priority. Ironically, when leaders accept the call to lead a team, or an organization, engaging with employees and expressing that commitment to them barely warrants mentioning. Of course, you'll engage the people you've been entrusted to lead and develop.

However, all too often, as responsibilities mount, employee engagement becomes less and less a priority and gets placed on the back burner. As the face of the company managing the frontline, leadership can shift that lack of enthusiasm by making minimal, deliberate, and consistent adjustments.

Rules of Engagement

Primarily, leaders need to be mindful of the words they choose. When offering performance feedback to an employee, share what *to do* rather than what *not to do*. Speaking in the affirmative can seem like a simple shift, but it's the positivity in your approach that your teams will appreciate.

Also, listen to your employees with your ears and eyes. See them; their posture, how they carry themselves, their facial expressions, what makes them laugh or even roll their eyes. All of this information, though non-verbal, is communicating something. And of course, spoken communication is helpful too. Say good morning, good afternoon, and good evening. Ask them how their lunch was. Ask them what they thought of the last staff meeting – did they have any questions or ideas they didn't get to ask? Listen thoughtfully to their responses. Once the ice is broken, you'll find that most people will open up without much prodding.

Empower your team to vent if they're having a particularly rough day, and then demonstrate empathy. Ask them what they need to do their job to the best of their ability? Take the time to know your employees' "why." What is their motivation? Are they motivated? As leaders, it's vital to know the answers to these questions for every team member: "Why are you here?" " How does our company fit into your life plan and aspirations?" "What are your aspirations... and what part can I play in helping you reach those goals?"

Asking these and other questions like them with sincere interest will make you a better leader. And it will create a stronger bond with your team. Last, and at the risk of stating the obvious, TALK to your team. Regularly. Communication is vital to any relationship, but uniquely so in a work environment. Lack of adequate communication can cause ripple effects in an organization that can have expensive ramifications.

Reasons to Engage

When engagement is a priority, employees feel valued and vital. When employees feel valued, they take more pride in their work performance. And when expectations are clearly and routinely defined by leaders, employees are less uncertain about their purpose within a company, and they step up to challenges more readily; trust and confidence in their leadership are fostered, and employees are generally happier coming to work.

Communicate the Vision

Indeed, you should offer feedback about a team member's performance, but don't just speak to them when it's evaluation time. Tell them who you are, why you're there, and what you've learned in your career (Li, 2015). Set aside time to reaffirm the company's vision as often as possible. When leaders communicate with their employees, your company's vision is at the core of that communication. Make sure teammates know that what they do and how well they do it has purpose and value to the organization's larger vision. Long-term satisfaction is less about compensation and more about being on the team and part of something important (Li, 2015).

Always at the forefront of leadership's mind should be the growth of their teams and the strengthening of the capabilities of individuals who make the team more effective. Leaders who lay this as their foundation create a space of continuous innovation and employee initiative. Remember, as leaders in today's business environment, you are in the energy business – the human energy business. Every leader must be intentional and consistent about creating a workplace where teammates can feel energized and not invisible.

Exercise

Give your team members notecards and ask them to answer the following question: In 2-3 sentences, "What is our organization's purpose?" Collect the cards and read them aloud. What do they tell you? Are answers similar, aligned to a common purpose, or are they all over the place? Consider the team's accuracy score reflecting your leadership and communication ability. Is there room for improvement? If so, include your team in the following steps to develop a more apparent organizational purpose that everyone can fully understand.

18. Adapt

Introduction

In the 1980s, with the commercialization of the internet, the world as we knew it, and certainly as our parents and grandparents knew it, began to turn on its head. The internet revolutionized everything we did, from what we ate, to what we bought, to how we developed social and business relationships, and even how we learned. The internet infiltrated every facet of modern life almost overnight.

By the early 2000s, social media began to upend the way we communicate entirely. According to the Pew Research Center, by 2011, 35% of Americans owned a tiny, high-powered computer called a smartphone, which put an endless stream of information, entertainment, and human consciousness in our pockets and at our fingertips. By 2019 that number had jumped to 96%. Business models that have existed since 1914 have been so wholly revamped and reimagined that they barely resemble their former selves. In 2021, experts estimate that nearly 85% of the jobs today's learners will be doing in 2030 haven't even been invented (Dwoskin, 2019). The ability to adapt is not optional; it's an urgent necessity.

The only constant in life is changes. In business, change is especially unavoidable. Companies must innovate to have continued growth. Therefore, leaders with fresh perspectives and innovative solutions will remain the lifeblood of how businesses continue to grow and evolve with the times.

To Be or Not To Be

Functioning adaptability is said to be made up of 2 components: flexibility and versatility. Using mistakes or failures as motivation to try different approaches until you are successful is an example of being both flexible and versatile. Flexibility refers to one's attitude and willingness to change. Versatility refers to one's capacity to change (Tan, et al., 2016). Leaders should encourage a tone of resiliency; adaptability and resilience are closely related qualities fundamental to business success. Indeed, when Charles Darwin said, "Survival of the fittest," he did not mean the quickest, the strongest, or the most intelligent life forms; instead, he was referring to those that were most capable of adapting to their environmental conditions (Business New Daily Editor, 2020).

If the prospect of experiencing the unexpected creates anxiety and insecurity in an employee, it may be difficult to have success. If an employee clings stubbornly to an inflexible attitude toward change, this individual may endearingly be a "creature of habit," but these individuals are just rendering themselves obsolete (Tan, et al., 2016).

(Getting) Ready For the World to Change

So, how do business leaders, professionals, and employees prepare for the world, so they are not entirely blindsided? First, it's essential that, as leaders and stakeholders, we review the company business plan and ensure it is aging well and keeping up with the times. Or does it need fine-tuning? Every project needs fine-tuning now and again. As industries evolve, so should the company's objectives. And as new challenges reveal themselves, so should the company's business plan be updated and adapted to detail the proper solutions. Every business plan should be a living document and be adjusted accordingly. Set new goals and objectives, and then reverse engineer your new plan step by step (Dwoskin, 2019).

To remain relevant in business, investing time and resources in your people is extremely important. Assembling and training the right people for the correct positions is critical. In the training and development environment, notice the individuals who best leverage their ability to adapt by being purposeful and deliberate about getting better at what they do, who consistently improve at levels greater and faster, and who think outside the box as opposed to those who haphazardly go through the motions of repetition, with no straightforward approach to getting better; those who express anxiety about the future or who are resistant to change. Their long-term prospects with the company may be slim. As simple as this sounds, the concept of deliberate practice has enormous implications for learning and developing professionals (Harward, 2018).

As your team is assembled, implement your evolved business plan by positioning your team. Whether by lateral or vertical promotion, prime and set your team for success by placing them in roles that suit their skills, their business needs, and their gifts. Be open with them about the evolving business plan and listen for their feedback. They are in the thick of it and will most likely see change before you do. Their perspective can give you the insight you need to prepare for future changes (Dwoskin, 2019).

Also, never hesitate to get to know new talent, individuals with fresh perspectives who aren't afraid to challenge the status quo. Remember ABR, *always be recruiting*. Interview even when you don't have positions open. There's always the possibility of a team member's life's circumstances changing or finding other employment, and rather than being reactive, always looking for exceptional talent (Dwoskin, 2019).

Human Resources

Technology and innovation in our modern world make work more streamlined and efficient with more minor errors. However, technology is still no match for the human imagination and judgment – at least not yet. Though the business world and the world at large might be amid metamorphosis in this newest Information Age, organizations still thrive on people's sweat equity and dedication. There is still no suitable substitute for human capital.

Being adaptable just means being flexible and maintaining a positive attitude through change. By remaining positive, we retain autonomy and control over our mindset and work environment (Business New Daily Editor, 2020).

Exercise

Survivor: Divide participants into two teams and present them with a survival situation: a plane crash, a shipwreck, lost in the desert. Then give them a list of items that might be useful in that situation. Challenge the groups to choose five things that will help them survive. After the teams finish picking their articles, ask them to justify their selections and how they would use those items to overcome their given circumstance. This leadership activity stimulates critical, creative, and strategic thinking and problem-solving skills that can be useful in your business.

Reference: The Sling Team "The 12 Best Leadership Activities To Help Develop Your Team's Skills" https://getsling.com/blog/ leadership-activities/

19. Deliver

Introduction

There is nothing more gratifying than when a plan comes together. When a project with many moving parts works together in harmony, and the hard work of planning, organizing, and execution pays off, it is a relief and thrilling at the same time. Replacement because everything that could have gone wrong didn't. Thrilling because a concept that may have only existed on paper, in one's imagination, or the collective dreams of a team has come to fruition and become a winner.

But what happens when a plan doesn't quite come together? Despite all efforts to the contrary, things are not adding up, and as it stands, commitments are on the verge of not being kept. What then? The truth is, these are the moments when leaders prove what caliber of leader they are. When the ramifications of a missed objective are fully realized, leaders know that their team could be adversely impacted. Perhaps they will have to release a team member if the goal is not met. Maybe the company's reputation is at stake and would receive irreversible damage if the commitment is not kept. What then?

What kind of leader are you? How do you show up for your team when there's been a setback? Are you the leader who will hold yourself accountable to your commitments with a pure desire to succeed and deliver? Do you take meeting objectives seriously for your team and your professional reputation? Or are you the kind of leader who accepts the easy route of mediocrity, who perhaps just makes excuses or outright chooses failure by quitting? In so many ways, a leader is not a leader until they face themself and ask these questions – and then answer them.

Time to Recalibrate and Adapt

When faced with an objective as a leader and you realize you are not where you want to be, it's always important to remind yourself of how you have gotten to that uncomfortable position. Retracing your steps and taking a second and third look at your plan to assess where things have gone wrong is critical to correcting the error and moving forward (Fox, 2017). Seek feedback from trusted colleagues on why they think things have gone wrong. Where and when exactly was the setback?

If there was a miscalculation or misinformation that was the flaw in the plan, as leaders, we must own that. If there was a communication breakdown along the way that caused a mistake, we must acknowledge that as leaders. The team you assemble is your responsibility. The work being done should be done under your watchful eye. Yes, mistakes happen, but a heart-centered leader takes ownership of the team's losses and salutes the team for their wins. A great leader creates value in the error by making it a lesson to prevent similar future missteps.

Leaders Who Deliver Make Bridges, Not Excuses

Now that the old plan has been broken down and the flaw diagnosed, it's time to rally the troops, bring your team back to the drawing board, and immediately instill confidence that this objective can and WILL be achieved. Your team must know you are willing to get your hands dirty to ensure the goal is accomplished. Standout performers on the team (perhaps future leaders) will be inspired and go beyond what is required.

Help your team connect what they've done well so far and where there's room for improvement. Review wins and losses with equal passion and discipline (Chan, 2018). Empower your team by letting them know that their skill sets and talents are particularly suited to execute this task.

Their leader must regularly remind a team that their work has purpose and value. Share as much detail as possible about the improved plan or process. Then delegate work based on priorities, results-oriented leaders use their position thoughtfully and vigilantly.

Leaders Who Deliver Are Motivators

Remember that possibly not meeting an objective can also be incredibly deflating and disheartening for that team. Among team members, emotions may run high as a result of disappointment. Tempers may flare as colleagues point fingers about what went wrong. Some team members may even express frustration if the objective is new and they aren't entirely confident in their abilities.

This is why it is of the utmost value that employees witness their leader maintain a good, positive, "can-do" attitude, especially in difficult moments. In managing your emotions and leading by example, a leader can single-handedly reshape the energy of a team and bring their focus back to the objectives at hand. This earns their respect, develops trust, inspires hope, and encourages them to remain positive.   Heart-centered leaders know a huge part of their responsibility to the team is to motivate and build up their team through these challenging moments.

Check in with your team members to ask, "What do you need right now to do your job to the best of your ability?" Then, listen to their response. Let them know you are willing to remove any barrier necessary so that they can achieve their fullest potential. It is incredibly motivating when employees feel their needs are being heard and prioritized. It also lets them know you believe in their abilities and want to support them.

Execute and Deliver

Now that the time has been invested in empowering and reinvigorating your team to face the tasks ahead, it's time to do just that. Strengthen communication; clearly define the plan and deploy the strategy by connecting it to individual actions. Use time wisely and efficiently. Embody the vision and see it through. The team is emboldened and even more, knowledgeable to be like Nike and *Just Do It*! Leaders who deliver are those of high moral fabric, discipline, and commitment. When stakes are high and challenges arise, these are the best kinds of leaders to have to lead your team.

Exercise

According to Dr. Barbara Fredrickson's Broaden-and-Build Theory (2001), positive emotions can help broaden your momentary thoughts, actions, and attention to your surroundings. One example of this is to foster positive thoughts and feelings. Says Fredrickson, the author of "Positivity" (2009): "In our research program, we found that the daily repertoire of emotions of people who are highly resilient is remarkably different from those who are not."   Consider ending your day by reflecting on and writing down three good things that happened.   Be intentional about reflecting on the experiences, noting how you felt, and what were three good things about the incident.

Reference: "Three Good Things Activity"

https://positivepsychology.com/resilience-activities-exercises/

Thank You

We want to say, "Thank you in advance for what you are about to encounter with heart-centered leadership." Through decades of discovering the wonders and complexities of leadership, we know all too well how difficult it can be to shift our hearts and minds.

But, because you have taken the time to read this guide and hopefully will take advantage of our other resources, we believe you are well on your way towards your transformational journey; and we know your teams will thank you!

Heart Work Profile® Assessment

The Heart Work Profile® opens up a self-exploratory journey for leaders, peeling back the layers of recovery and opening hearts and minds to discovery. This experience reveals the critical importance of leading with love in all that one does. Scan the QR code and learn more about the Heart Work Profile®.

Heart Work Facilitator - Leadership Professional®

Becoming a Heart Work Facilitator - Leadership Professional® (HWF-LP®) equips heart-centered leaders with the insight, critical knowledge, and know-how to implement the Heart Work Profile® and thoughtfully create business systems, operations, and cultures that reflect LOVE. And when leaders intentionally design businesses with LOVE, business excellence becomes inevitable. Scan the QR code and learn more about the HWF-LP®.

REFERENCES

1. Di Fabio, A., Palazzeschi, L., & Bucci, O. (2017) Gratitude in organizations: A contribution for healthy organizational contexts. Frontiers in Psychology, 8, 2025. https://doi.org/10.3389/fpsyg.2017.02025

2. Integrated Benefits Institute (2018) https://www.ibiweb.org/poor-health-costs-us-employers-530-billion-and-1-4-billion-

3. Fairview Health Services (2017) https://www.fairview.org/blog/8-Amazing-Benefits-of-the-Simple-Thank-You

4. Heubeck, E. (2004) Boost your health with a dose of gratitude: If you want to get healthier, give thanks. WebMD. https://www.webmd.com/women/features/gratitute-health-boost#1

5. Dunn, L. (2015) Be thankful: Science says gratitude is good for your health. Today. https://www.today.com/health/be-thankful-science-says-gratitude-good-your-health-t58256

6. Mosley, E. (2019) The business impact of gratitude. Forbes. https://www.forbes.com/sites/ericmosley/2019/11/27/the-business-impact-of-gratitude/?sh=6f42f976630c

7. Nawaz, S. (2020) In times of crisis, a little thanks goes a long way. Harvard Business Review. https://hbr.org/2020/05/in-times-of-crisis-a-little-thanks-goes-a-long-way?ab=hero- main-text

8. Craig, N. and Snook, S. (2014) From purpose to impact: Figure out your passion and put it to work. Harvard Business Review. https://static1.squarespace.com/static/5918d0d6d482e97b75495c93/t/593210b7440 24303f35d1b35/1496453306161/From+Purpose+to+Impact-+HBR+May+2014.pdf

9.   Hedges, K. (2018) Don't have a leadership vision? Here's where to find it. Forbes Women. https://www.forbes.com/sites/work-in-progress/2018/10/25/dont-have-a-leadership-v ision-heres-where-to-find-it/?sh=71239a9a0a8a

10.   Tourish, D. (2020) Introduction to the special issue: Why the coronavirus is also a crisis of leadership. Sage Publishing. https://journals.sagepub.com/doi/full/10.1177/1742715020929242#

11.   Johnson, A. (2014) Why love is the first leadership skill you should develop: Return on values feature. https://cvdl.ben.edu/blog/love-leadership-skill-develop-return-values-feature/

12.   Coombe, D. (2016) Can you really power an organization with love? Harvard Business Review. https://hbr.org/2016/08/can-you-really-power-an-organization-with-love

13.   Anderson, V., Caldwell, C., and Barfuss, B. (2019) Love: The heart of leadership. Graziado Business Review. https://gbr.pepperdine.edu/2019/08/love-the-heart-of-leadership/

14.   (2020) Center for Creative Leadership. A Leader's Best Bet: Exercise. https://www.ccl.org/articles/leading-effectively-articles/spotlight-on-exercise-and-leadership/

15.   Purcell, J. (2016) Employers Need to Recognize That Our Wellness Starts at Work. https://hbr.org/2016/11/employers-need-to-recognize-that-our-wellness-starts-at-work

16.   Kurland, M (2020) Prioritize Health And Wellness For Yourself And Your Team. https://www.forbes.com/sites/theyec/2020/07/01/prioritize-health-and-wellness-for-yourself- and-your-team/?sh=757e4da750c9

17.   IMD. https://www.imd.org/research-knowledge/articles/resilient-leadership-navigating-the-pressu res-of-modern-working-life/

18.   Gavin, M. (2019) How to become a more resilient leader. Harvard
        Business School Online. https://online.hbs.edu/blog/post/resilient-
        leadership

19.   Smith, C. (2015) How coaching helps leadership resilience: The
        leadership perspective. International Coaching Psychology Review I Vol.
        10 No. 1.

20.   Doll, K. (2021) 23 Resilience Building Tools and Exercises (+ Mental
        Toughness Test) https://positivepsychology.com/resilience-activities-
        exercises/

21.   3 exercises to elevate your leadership presence. https://
        hernewstandard.com/3-exercises-to-elevate-your-leadership-presence/

22.   Gray, K. (2018) "What Is Professional Presence and How Can I Achieve
        It?" Columbia Business School. https://www8.gsb.columbia.edu/articles/
        columbia-business/what-professional-presence-and-how-can-i-achieve-it

23.   Schwartzberg, J. (2020) "How To Elevate Your Presence In A Virtual
        Meeting". Harvard Business Review. https://hbr.org/2020/04/how-to-
        elevate-your-presence-in-a-virtual-meeting

24.   Goman, C.K. (2016) 5 Ways to Instantly Increase Your Leadership
        Presence. Forbes. https://www.forbes.com/sites/carolkinseygoman/
        2016/01/18/5-ways-to-instantly-increase-your-leadership-presence/?
        sh=40b0ad5b3073

25.   Zwilling, M. (2016) 8 Reasons to Find Joy in Your Job. https://
        www.entrepreneur.com/article/274960

26.   Fabrega, M. 21 Ways to Create and Maintain a Positive Attitude. https://
        daringtolivefully.com/positive-attitude

27. Seedman, J. The Most Important Leadership Quality / Perseverance is Both Success & Failure's Best Friend as the Greatest Lessons Are Learned in the Valleys not the Peaks. https://www.pniconsulting.com/articles/persevere

28. Merriman, K. (2017) Leadership and Perseverance. 10.1007/978-3-319-31036-7_19. https://www.researchgate.net/publication/318034785_Leadership_and_Perseverance

29. Edblad, P. (2017) This Is How to Grow Your Grit: 5 Secrets from Research. https://betterhumans.pub/this-is-how-to-grow-your-grit-5-secrets-from-research-9c78c803093e

30. Kalloo, K. (2018) The Power of Perseverance for Leaders & Business Owners. https://www.changemybusinesscoaching.ca/2018/04/20/the-power-of-perseverance-for-leaders-business-owners/

31. Gottfredson, R. And Reina, C. (2020) Leadership and Managing People: To Be A Great Leader, You Need the Right Mindset. https://hbr.org/2020/01/to-be-a-great-leader-you-need-the-right-mindset?registration=success

32. Clark, L. (2020) Leadership Development: Mind Over Matter: Leadership Mindsets and Actions to Drive Results. https://www.chieflearningofficer.com/2020/02/19/mind-over-matter-leadership-mindsets-and-actions-to-drive-results/

33. Gleeson, B. (2018) 7 Mindsets Necessary For Successful Leadership Development. https://www.forbes.com/sites/brentgleeson/2018/05/31/7-mindsets-necessary-for-successful-leadership-development/?sh=4acf0d4e50d3

34. Sime, C. (2019) The Cost of Ignoring Mental Health in the Workplace. https://www.forbes.com/sites/carleysime/2019/04/17/the-cost-of-ignoring-mental-health-in-the-workplace/?sh=168f50633726

35. Morin, A. (2020) How to Improve Your Psychological Well Being. https://www.verywellmind.com/improve-psychological-well-being-4177330

36. Lipkin, N. (2020) Workforce Wellbeing: Supporting the Emotional Wellness of Employees and Teams. https://trainingindustry.com/articles/compliance/workforce-well-being-supporting-the-emotional-wellness-of-employees-and-teams/

37. Meurer, M. (2017) Our world is changing at 10x speed: How to prepare and be the change! https://www.huffpost.com/entry/our-world-is-changing-at-10x-speed-how-to-prepare_b_59a55415e4b0d6cf7f405027

38. Dwoskin, J, (2019) Adaptability Is The Key To Business Growth: Five Ways To Stay Ahead Of Real-Time. https://www.forbes.com/sites/forbescoachescouncil/2019/12/09/adaptability-is-the-key-to-business-growth-five-ways-to-stay-ahead-of-real-time/?sh=63b4e71e428d

39. Tan, S. (2016) How Well Do You Handle Change? The Benefits of Being Adaptable. https://www.business.com/articles/how-well-do-you-handle-change-the-benefits-of-being-adaptable/

40. Business News Daily Editor (2020) Stay Positive! Resilient and Adaptable Teams are Key to Business Success. https://www.businessnewsdaily.com/10157resilienceadaptabilitybusinesssuccess.html#:~:text=Business%20is%20constantly%20changing%2C%20and,and%20maintaining%20a%20positive%20attitude

41.   Chaffold, J. (2020) 4 Leadership Listening Skills of Top Managers.
      https://www.insperity.com/blog/4-must-use-listening-techniques-
      leaders/

42.   Toledo, M. (2018) Business Tolls: The Art of Listening. https://
      www.forbes.com/sites/forbeslacouncil/2018/05/30/business-tools-the-
      art-of-listening/?sh=581cac8b26b1

43.   Tingum, J. (2019) Why Is Listening Important in a Business
      Organization? https://smallbusiness.chron.com/listening-important-
      business-organisation-24040.html

44.   Raab, D. (2019) What is Emotional Wellness? https://
      www.psychologytoday.com/us/blog/the-empowerment-diary/201910/
      what-is-emotional-wellness

45.   Curtis, O. (2017) How Mental Wellness Can Boost The Bottom Line - The
      impact of mental wellness in the workplace. https://
      www.gnapartners.com/resources/news/how-mental-wellness-can-boost-
      the-bottom-line

46.   Kohll, A. (2018) 5 Reasons Social Connections Can Enhance Your
      Employee Wellness Program. https://www.forbes.com/sites/alankohll/
      2018/01/31/5-ways-social-connections-can-enhance-your-employee-
      wellness-program/?sh=2bd71190527c

47.   Jackson, M. (2020) Build a Company Culture That Prioritizes Social
      Wellness. https://www.recruiter.com/i/build-a-company-culture-that-
      prioritizes-social-wellness/
      #:~:text=If%20your%20organization%20implements%20a,in%20the%
      20war%20for%20talent.

48.   Amador de San Jose, C. (2019) How to Address the 7 Dimensions of
        Wellness in the Workplace. https://allwork.space/2019/05/how-to-
        address-the-7-dimensions-of-wellness-in-the-workplace/
        #:~:text=Social%20wellness%20is%20about%20building,other%20co
        workers%20and%20staff%20members.

49.   Optimum Performance Institute (2013) 7 Ways to Successfully Cultivate
        Social Wellness For Life. https://
        www.optimumperformanceinstitute.com/life-coaching/7-ways-to-
        successfully-cultivate-social-wellness-for-life
        #:~:text=What%20is%20social%20wellness%3F,the%20bigger%20puz
        zle%20of%20humankind.

50.   Bevacqua, J. (2019) Social Well-being, Wellness and Connection in the
        Workplace. https://risepeople.com/blog/social-wellness-in-the-
        workplace/

51.   Fox, B.A. (2017) Don't Give Up, Deliver: Overcoming a Setback to Deliver
        Results. https://bonnieartmanfox.com/dont-give-deliver-overcoming-
        setback-deliver-results/

52.   Chan, S. (2018) Leaders Who Destroy vs Leaders Who Deliver. https://
        simonchan.co/leaders-destroy-vs-leaders-deliver/

53.   Kaufman Global. A Committed Leader: The Key Ingredient for
        Change. https://www.kaufmanglobal.com/committed-leader-leading-
        change/

54.   Dam, R. And Siang, Teo Yu (2021) 5 Stages in Design Thinking Process.
        https://www.interaction-design.org/literature/article/5-stages-in-the-
        design-thinking-process

55.   White, A. (2020) How to Implement Design Thinking In Your Workplace.
        https://standardbeagle.com/implementing-design-
        thinking#:~:text=It%20is%20important%20to%20implement,solving%
        20problems%20based%20on%20assumptions.&text=Think%20of%20
        design%20thinking%20as%20a%20methodology%20for%20creative%
        20problem%2Dsolving.

56.   Daskal, L . 26 Qualities That Will Lead You to Greatness. https://
        www.lollydaskal.com/leadership/26-qualities-will-lead-greatness/

57.   Campbell, S. (2018) 6 Qualities of Greatness. https://
        www.entrepreneur.com/article/309995

58.   Campbell, S. (2015) Develop These 7 Habits To Unlock Your Greatness.
        https://www.entrepreneur.com/article/254492

59.   Glaser, J. (2016) When 'Heart Intelligence' meets 'Conversational
        Intelligence. https://www.vistage.com/research-center/business-
        leadership/20161004-when-heart-intelligence-meets-conversational-
        intelligence/

60.   (2015) The Heart - An Agent of Transformation. https://
        www.heartmath.org/articles-of-the-heart/heartmath-tools-techniques/
        heart-agent-transformation/

61.   (2012) Heart Intelligence. https://www.heartmath.org/articles-of-the-
        heart/the-math-of-heartmath/heart-intelligence/

62.   Li, C. (2015) 3 Things All Engaged Leaders Have In Common. https://
        www.fastcompany.com/3043688/3-things-all-engaged-leaders-have-in-
        common

63.   LLopis, G. (2015) 6 Things Wise Leaders Do To Engage Their Employees.
        https://www.forbes.com/sites/glennllopis/2015/02/02/6-things-wise-
        leaders-do-to-engage-their-employees/?sh=58527b697f5d

64.   Davis, B. (2014) Educational Reform: Ten Exercises in Heart Intelligence
       https://www.huffpost.com/entry/school-days-again-ten-exe_b_5600857

65.   Taylor, V. (2015) Unhappy in America: Nearly 70% of U.S. employees
       miserable at work, study finds. http://www.nydailynews.com/life-style/
       majority-u-s-workers-not-engaged-job-gallup-poll-article-1.2094990

Made in the USA
Columbia, SC
30 November 2022